Dark of the Moon

Lying in bed, Judy saw the pale full moon through the half-open window. Outside, the sounds of the city had died to a few gentle murmurs, like those of a giant animal in uneasy sleep.

But sleep would not come to Judy. Images filled her mind . . . the fear-frozen face of her murdered friend . . . the mysterious briefcase no one could find . . . the men and women who regarded Judy with such hate . . . Jonathan, who promised so much, concealed so much . . .

Suddenly the moon was behind a cloud. Suddenly all was dark. Suddenly Judy knew she was no longer alone in the room, and that there was—

NO HIDING PLACE

No Hiding Place

RAE FOLEY

A DELL BOOK

Published by
DELL PUBLISHING CO., INC.
750 Third Avenue
New York, New York 10017
Copyright © 1969 by Rae Foley
Dell ® TM 681510, Dell Publishing Co., Inc.
Reprinted by arrangement with
Dodd, Mead & Company
New York, New York
Printed in the United States of America
First Dell printing—June 1971

1

"Don't look now," the woman said, "I am being watched." She added, "But please listen to me."

Above the rumble of the train it was difficult to make out her words. Judy, carefully folding her newspaper into the smallest possible compass, a trick she had acquired during her first week of subway riding, risked a glance at the passenger beside her, whose eyes seemed to be engrossed in the paper she held, almost covering her face. Her lips barely moved but she was, indubitably, speaking to Judy.

She didn't look insane, though of course you couldn't always tell, but she was certainly hagridden. She was in her middle or late fifties, with badly dyed red hair, thickly made-up eyes that squinted at the newsprint as though she needed glasses and refused to surrender to them. There were dark pouches under the tired eyes and long deep grooves like scars in her cheeks.

Judy knew about the scars. Only the night before her knowledgeable roommate had drawn her attention to a woman seated in front of them at the theater. Those deep grooves, Peg had explained, were what sometimes happened after a face-lifting job if the person could not afford to follow up with a second.

The woman's mouth moved again as though she were reading to herself. "Don't look at me. Just listen." She added, with a touch of panic in that stifled voice, "Are you listening?"

Judy spoke to her folded newspaper. "Yes." Her own voice was little more than a breath, but the woman's hand relaxed its tight grip on her paper.

"I need help," she said, her voice still low but distinct. Somewhere she had learned how to articulate beautifully.

She's mad, Judy decided. Peg's always warning me not to get involved with crackpots. This is where I clear out. She started to pick up her briefcase, which was wedged between her and the oddball.

"No," the woman whispered. "Please. Oh, God! Please."

Turning her paper, refolding it, Judy muttered, "What do you want?"

"Take my briefcase and leave yours. They look alike. I'll—if I get away, if I get out of this jam, I'll advertise for mine in the Lost and Found of the *Times*. There will be an adequate reward. If I don't make it, you can do as you see fit. It won't matter then. Just take it away. That's my only chance."

The train was slowing down and people were beginning their inexorable pressure toward the doors, trying to compress two bodies into the space of one, as though a second's time might be gained by this mass discomfort.

"Times Square," the woman said. "I implore you. Go! Go quickly. In this mob we'll have our best chance to get away." There was a white line around her mouth, her upper lip glistened with perspiration.

Something of the woman's stark terror communicated itself to Judy. Jammed and buffeted by the pushing crowd, she stood up, lifting the briefcase that had been propped beside her own. She let the shoving crowd move her toward the side door, and the pressure behind her shot her out onto the platform like a cork out of a bottle of champagne, stumbling, finding it difficult to regain her balance before being swept onto the express tracks. Then she was moving toward the stairs, hemmed in by the crowd, the briefcase clutched in her hand. She had no way of telling whether or not the other woman was following her.

Out on Forty-second Street the summer heat made her reel. The day had been hot, but now it seemed even

2

hotter, more breathless. The ruthless glare of the sun was reflected back by steel and glass buildings, it rose up from underground trains, pressed down from a brassy sky, was shut in by long narrow canyons.

She stopped for a moment to get her bearings. She was still so much a newcomer in New York that whenever she emerged from a different exit at Times Square, she had to reconnoiter to find out where she was.

For a moment she absorbed the impact of throbbing motors, the heat from exhausts, as bumper-to-bumper traffic moved along Forty-second Street. An electric sign running around a building provided the cheering news that the day's heat had struck a new record. Beyond were the gigantic signs on Broadway, their garish lights dimmed by the sun.

Judy turned west toward the Port Authority Bus Terminal. Unlike the briefcase she had carried all day, this one was unexpectedly heavy and she wondered why on earth she had responded to the woman's desperate appeal by saddling herself with the thing. Peg would tell her that she had been a fool. Peg, it occurred to her belatedly, might also be annoyed, and justifiably so, because the briefcase Judy had been carrying was her roommate's property.

There was the shrill, sickening sound of sirens as police cars tore past, their roof lights blinking. Somebody was in trouble.

The usual commuting throng was piling into the big bus terminal. Judy shifted the heavy briefcase from one hand to the other while she gripped the rail of the steep escalator. There would be a bus leaving for Danbury, Connecticut, in four minutes. In spite of the sweltering heat, Judy ran for it. Always it seemed that the bus she wanted was in the farthest lane. She joined the line that had already formed and was lucky enough to get a seat. She leaned back panting while other passengers came down the aisle, found seats, and removed jackets, though this bus, fortunately, was air-conditioned.

Beside hers another crowded bus moved off, headed

3

for Connecticut or New Jersey, Washington, D.C., or Boston, or perhaps some remote part of the United States a thousand or two thousand or three thousand miles away. Judy wondered when she would become accustomed to the fact that everyone in America seemed to be going somewhere on wheels. At least she had learned not to express her wonder aloud. Lack of sophistication was not highly esteemed in the set to which Peg was initiating her, and Judy was still young enough to prefer being boiled in oil to making a laughingstock of herself. Anyhow, she owed it to Peg to create as good an impression as possible.

Now and then, it occurred to her that she owed a great deal to her roommate, more than she felt comfortable about owing anyone. Not that Peg ever hinted at the extent of her obligation, ever mentioned that she paid the rent of the apartment she shared with Judy; that she had carried all their joint expenses in the month since Judy had come to New York at her suggestion; that the friends and the parties had all been Peg's, even the dates had been with men who had come originally to see Peg.

Just the same, though Judy felt disloyal for her sense of escape, it was a relief to get away for a few days, to go home by herself for the closing of the sale of her small cottage outside Danbury. Considering the amount for which she had had to mortgage it to meet her father's medical expenses during his last illness, there wouldn't be much left, perhaps only three or four thousand dollars. Still she could live independently on that until she landed a suitable job.

Up to now she had limited herself to applying for jobs on magazines, in television studios, and radio stations, because they would obviously be glamorous. If she couldn't become famous, she might at least look at famous people. She had been somewhat taken aback to discover that the same idea had occurred to countless other young women from the country, who had arrived in New York equipped, like herself, with nothing but stenographic skills and a taste for glamour.

4

When she went back to the city tomorrow, Judy decided, she would go farther afield. She would not depend so much on Peg, who had done her best to help her land a job on a magazine. Peg herself worked as a researcher for *New Trends,* though she had never been able to explain to the literal Judy exactly what a new trend was when you met one.

The briefcase had been Peg's idea. "It has such a nice official look," she said. "You might already be working at something terrible important."

"Don't you need it yourself?"

"Not today."

"Anything in it?"

"Just my name and address, in the unlikely case it should be found somewhere by an honest man."

"Oh, Peg," Judy had protested, "don't you trust anyone?"

Peg had looked at her rather oddly. "Only you."

I'll have to buy Peg a new briefcase when I get back to town on Monday, Judy thought guiltily, and gathered up the one the woman on the subway had thrust on her. But what I'm supposed to do with this, only heaven knows.

II

It was hot in Danbury, but not as hot as in Manhattan. In the parking lot Judy unlocked her little Renault and gasped with the heat as she rolled down the windows and cautiously touched the wheel, blistering in the sun in which it had baked, day after day, during the past month. As soon as she had run out of town onto a typical Connecticut country road, narrow, winding, tree-lined, she began to cool off.

There were very few cars on this road in midweek after the office and factory workers had gone home. Distant hillsides were thickly green. There was still plenty of water in the reservoirs and streams. Corn was high in a field. A pheasant strolling across the highway

5

refused to accelerate its leisurely pace, and Judy braked to a stop.

"You're just asking for it," she called, but the bird went on its meditative way, fancy-free.

Half a mile along a dirt road there was a steep gravel driveway and the little car made it in low gear. Judy hoped the new owners would have good brakes, and stifled a pang of envy. Only a deep but unstated need for independence had made her put the little cottage on the market, even when she knew it was the sensible, indeed the inevitable, thing to do. She had to earn a living and she needed this backlog to keep her going if she were not to be completely dependent on Peg.

She took the house key from her handbag, rejoicing that she had disregarded Peg's advice to have the electricity and water and telephone services shut off. "Sheer extravagance when you aren't using them," Peg had said severely, spraying herself with perfume at $20 an ounce.

The cottage was pleasantly cool because the windows and blinds had been closed against the sun and the heat. And it was silent. Of course it was always quiet here in the hills, in the woods.

Then, as Judy turned the light switch beside the door, the silence was shattered by the shrilling of the telephone. Peg making sure she got home all right. No one else knew she was going to spend this last night alone in the cottage before it belonged to someone else.

"Hello," she said. "I made it all right. What a worry-wort you are!"

"Made what?" inquired a man's voice.

"Oh, you must have the wrong number."

"I know how to dial," the man said rather crossly. "Isn't this Miss Morrison?"

"Peg? No."

"Are you expecting her?"

"No. Who is this?"

"Are you the girl who shares her apartment? Judith Wilkins?"

"Yes."

"Well, where the hell is Miss Morrison?"

"I don't know where she is if she isn't at the apartment."

"She isn't. I've called half a dozen times and left messages at the switchboard. Then I remembered that she mentioned you and your cottage and said you'd be going up there. She expected to be home by six. We had a date for six o'clock."

"Have you tried *New Trends?* She probably wouldn't be there so late, but that's where she works."

"I know where she works," said the man with the short temper. "They lent her to me this morning for a couple of weeks of research. She was also going to do some interviewing. They tell me she's a natural at it. Then she was to call me at six and we'd go over the stuff she had picked up and decide on the next step. Now I'm in the hell of a spot. He's not the kind of guy you call and ask to give you the stuff all over again. It may take weeks to arrange another appointment. I seem to be stymied. Do you have any ideas?"

"No, I haven't. And I don't like it one bit, Mr.—uh—"

"Fullbright," he said shortly.

"Peg makes a fetish of promptness. Do you think something has happened to her?"

"Why should it? Take my number, will you, just in case you hear from her."

Judy wrote it down carefully. "Though there's not any reason why she would call me. I can't understand her not keeping an appointment unless she was involved in an accident or she was overcome by the heat today. Do you suppose she could possibly be ill in the apartment and unable to come to the telephone?"

"How the—" he began irritably, but the genuine anxiety in her voice reached him over the wire. "I'll go up there and check, if you like," he grumbled. "My plans for the evening seem to be shot anyhow." He slammed down the telephone before she could thank him.

Of all the impossible men, Judy thought. It was a

pity Peg had got involved with him. As a rule she had a talent for avoiding disagreeable or boring people, even if she had to be ruthless to do it. But she didn't walk out on her obligations. Ever. It was odd that she had not kept that appointment.

When she had showered, Judy stood surveying herself questioningly. She didn't have Peg's thin, elegant silhouette, she admitted, nor Peg's exquisite grooming, nor her air of cool, somewhat arrogant, distinction. She was a bit too rounded for high fashion, her ash-blond hair with its tight natural curl didn't lend itself to stylized hair setting, the freckles on her small nose couldn't be concealed by powder. She looked much younger than her twenty-two years.

In the beginning she had been afraid that she would never be able to fit in among Peg's sophisticated friends, but once she learned to keep still about things she didn't know, which Peg assured her was a very rare trait indeed, she seemed to do all right.

"It's that wide-eyed effect," Peg had told her, laughing. "To the men in the set I travel with it is devastating. And, of course, that damned naïve honesty of yours is taken for a novel kind of subtle wit."

It was curious that she could not stop thinking about Peg tonight. The telephone call from the irritable Mr. Fullbright had upset her. But there wasn't anything she could do. She went into the kitchen to explore the cupboard. There wasn't much in the way of supplies, as she had cleared things out before leaving the cottage. All that was left was the emergency shelf, stocked by Peg herself, the one time she had spent a weekend there. You simply had to be prepared for unexpected guests in the country, Peg had said.

Judy grinned as she saw the caviar, the lobster, the Newburg sauce, the tiny French peas. She got them out, set the table on the terrace, mixed a mild gin and tonic, added lime, and switched on the radio.

There was a cool breeze on the stone terrace behind the cottage, and she stretched out on a canvas chair, looking into the woods beyond the lawn, hearing the sleepy cheep of birds while they settled down for the night, the distant barking of an excited dog, the pleasant tinkle of ice against the tall glass. She sipped the long cold drink contentedly and was aware that the radio had warmed up and she was hearing the slow part of the Chopin Fantaisie-Impromptu. The music ended with a rush of sound, and a voice—now they all sounded like the Voice of Doom—enumerated the number of killed and wounded in a chain car accident; the effects of a cyclone in Kansas; an oil fire in Texas; a mass demonstration somewhere that, either deliberately or by accident, had stirred up violence and left its toll of injured.

"Service," the Voice of Doom went on, "has been resumed on the Broadway subway, which was halted for two hours when a woman jumped or fell onto the express tracks at Times Square at five o'clock. So far the victim, a red-haired woman in her late fifties, has not been identified. The temperature in Central Park at seven o'clock was—"

She didn't get away after all. That was the clearest thought Judy had. Up to now she had not really believed in the woman's danger, though she had not questioned her terror. She had been horribly afraid.

Look, Judy told herself impatiently, don't let yourself be carried away. Something terrible has happened and it comes close because the woman was speaking to you just a minute before she died. But perhaps it wasn't murder. After all, Judy herself had been expelled from the train so violently she had almost pitched across the platform onto the express tracks. It could be an accident. It probably was an accident. Or it could be another red-haired woman in her late fifties. It all sounded fine and Judy didn't believe a word of it.

What exactly had the woman said? "I'm being watched." And, without the briefcase, she would have a chance.

Judy got up stiffly and went in to switch off the radio and then stood staring at the briefcase. And what, she wondered, am I going to do about you now?

It was only belatedly that a picture began to take shape in her mind. The woman had not been identified, although she had been carrying the briefcase that contained Peg's name and address. And Peg had not kept a six o'clock appointment!

The ringing of the telephone made her leap like a startled deer. It was the Fullbright man again and this time he did not seem irritable. He was frankly dismayed by the task he had to perform, which was perhaps as well, because the shock and strain in his voice penetrated even before the meaning of his words, leaving Judy half prepared.

"Miss Wilkins, this is Jonathan Fullbright again. I am speaking from your apartment. Miss Morrison—"

"What happened to Peg?" Judy tried to keep her voice steady. "Did you—find her?"

"Yes, she's here. She—there's no easy way of telling you, I'm afraid. She is dead." Having got over the worst, he went on more quickly, "Evidently she walked in on a burglar. The apartment has been ransacked. He—seems to have knocked her on the head. I've called the police, of course, but I thought you ought to be advised."

"They must have been looking for the briefcase," Judy said dully. "I led them right to her."

"What are you talking about?"

"The red-haired woman on the subway. I just heard on the radio. They got her, too."

"You mean the one in the news tonight? The one who fell at Times Square?"

"She was pushed. I have her briefcase and that is why she was killed and why Peg is dead, and what in God's name am I to do?"

"I don't know what this is all about," the man Fullbright said, "but if I were you, I'd keep my trap shut until I knew the score."

"And what about the briefcase?"

"Hell, I don't know the plot. I just walked in at the end of the picture. Offhand, I'd say to get rid of the thing, whatever it is, and deny you ever saw it. And I haven't called you. Clear? All right, I can't talk any longer. I hear the police."

2

Judy found herself looking blankly at the dead telephone. Then, without bothering to change, without even having formulated a plan, she carried the briefcase out to the car, carefully negotiated the steep driveway, and followed the road back to Danbury. She had nothing in mind but an ungovernable impulse to get rid of the thing that had brought death to two women.

In Danbury she turned aimlessly toward the residential streets. There should be a garbage can, something. Then she saw the huge truck parked outside a house. There was no one in the truck, no one on the sidewalk, no one in sight in the house although the whole place was lighted and the door stood wide open. Inside she saw a trunk, a couple of boxes, a crate of some kind, although at that moment she was not even aware that she saw them.

She pulled up behind the truck, got out of the Renault, and thrust the briefcase inside the open back of the truck, under some sort of cover, and then, her heart lighter, she got back in the car, put on speed, turned the corner, and returned to the cottage.

The telephone was ringing as she went in but, in the perverse way telephones have, it stopped before she could reach it. She went out to the kitchen, scraped out her untouched supper, and finally heated water in which she dissolved a bouillon cube. She sipped it, walking up and down the room. Peg had been killed because her name was in the briefcase the red-haired woman had been carrying. They hadn't wasted much time. Judy shivered, although now that the breeze had died down, the evening was sultry.

The last of the color faded from the sky, but there were blinking lights on the road below, the roof lights of a police car. Then twin high beams came up the steep driveway like exploring fingers. A motor raced and a car door slammed.

Judy waited, her heart thudding. Minutes seemed to pass before there was a knock at the door. She opened it to a young state trooper who looked in surprise and evident approval at the small, but not too small, girl.

"I am looking for a Miss Wilkins," he said, smiling as though to reassure her. "Miss Judith Wilkins."

"I am Judith Wilkins." She wondered whether he could hear the thunder of her heart. "Won't you come in?"

"Well—yes, thank you." He was obviously not only taken aback by her youth but disturbed by it. She thought resentfully that he probably believed she was not more than seventeen. That had been the reaction of several people to whom she had applied for jobs.

"I," he cleared his throat, "that is, the New York police called us. That is, do you know a Margaret Morrison?" He seemed almost to hope that her answer would be in the negative.

Careful, Judy thought. "Why, yes, she is my roommate." As he looked around the small living room, she said, "Not here. I am sharing her apartment in New York, at least until I get settled somewhere on my own."

"Where is the apartment?"

She gave him the address of Peg's apartment in the East Fifties, surprised to hear how steady her voice sounded.

"I'm afraid I have bad news for you, Miss Wilkins. Your friend, Miss Morrison, was murdered late this afternoon at her apartment."

"Mur—"

"The apartment was pretty well torn apart. The New York men don't know, of course, what was taken."

Judy had dropped into a chair and sat staring at him. The state trooper was very good-looking; he was extremely pleasant and polite; he was also disturbingly observant. "They got your address at the desk in your apartment building. We tried to reach you several times, but you didn't answer your phone. Where have you been since—oh, say, five-thirty?"

"I must have been on the terrace," Judy said dazedly. Whatever she had expected, it had not been an inquiry by the police into her own movements. "With the radio on, I don't suppose I'd have heard the phone."

He was still polite, but his pleasant expression had changed. "You say you have been on your terrace since five-thirty this afternoon?"

"Oh, no! Just since I got home. I came up from New York on the five-fifteen bus to Danbury."

"Why?"

She was puzzled. "Well, I can't afford to garage the car in New York and—"

"No, I meant why did you come up here?"

"Oh, I came for the closing of the sale of my cottage tomorrow morning at ten. It was easier to come and spend the night than to catch an early bus in the morning."

"I suppose this appointment for closing the deal on the house is important, that it can't be put off."

"Not very well. The new owners plan to move in tomorrow, right after the closing. They probably have their stuff packed and waiting to be delivered, moving men engaged, all that."

"But you wouldn't mind returning to New York as soon as you've completed this deal?"

"Of course not. I intended to go back, anyhow. But why—"

"The police would be most grateful to you. Naturally they want to see you as quickly as possible. They had thought maybe tonight—but I'll explain about your appointment. Suppose I pick you up at your bank at— How long does it take? An hour?"

"I have no idea. It's the only time I ever sold anything."

"Suppose we say eleven." The trooper studied her as carefully as though he were counting the freckles on her short nose. "Of course you'll be eager to help us find out who killed your roommate."

"Well, of course."

"Were you old friends or did you meet recently in New York?"

"No, I've known Peg most of my life. Her people had a summer place on Lake Candlewood."

"What people?"

Judy shook her head. "There's no one left now. Her parents died several years ago and she never had any brothers or sisters."

"No one at all?"

"Well, there's a cousin. Maxwell something. I don't remember his last name. She—Peg never liked him much."

"And he is the only living relative you know of. Is that correct?"

"Yes."

"What about friends?"

"Peg doesn't—didn't have close friends. She—was rather aloof, detached from people. I knew her better than anyone but not really well because of the difference in our ages and then—we were so different generally."

"What about enemies?"

Judy shook her head. "Not Peg. I suppose people resented her now and then, but that's not—you don't kill people for that."

"Why would they resent her?"

"She didn't suffer fools. If she disliked people, she simply refused to bother with them. And she didn't have much faith in them. She never explained, but I think some time or other she had been engaged and found out something about the man. I don't really know."

15

"But she trusted you." He was smiling but his eyes were still too intent.

"Well, we got along, though she was nearly six years older. I think I—sort of amused her because she thinks," Judy gulped, "she thought I was awfully naïve."

"A person might get that impression," the trooper admitted, and he didn't sound as friendly as he had at first. "You say you didn't leave the cottage at all after you got here this evening? That would have been about when? Seven-thirty?"

"About that," Judy agreed. She recalled Peg warning her in amusement, "Never try to lie, Judy. You look so guilty and ashamed that you give yourself away every time." She remembered, too, that there had been a small interval between the time when the trooper's car had arrived and he had reached the door. Had he been examining the Renault to see whether or not the motor was warm?

"I had to go into town to get some food for supper," she said casually. "There wasn't a thing in the cottage, of course, as it has been closed up for a month and I forgot until I got here."

His face lightened. He seemed about to leave, then he asked, as though it were an afterthought, "Were you or your friend Miss Morrison in the habit of keeping money, jewelry, valuables of any kind, in the apartment?"

"I don't own any valuables," Judy said promptly. "Peg had some things, a few diamond rings and a pearl necklace of her mother's, but she didn't care about wearing jewelry, so it is left in the bank. And she never kept money in the apartment."

"Odd," he said. "That was the only apartment in the building to be broken into. They must have been looking for something. Or else—" He paused. "I take it your friend was fairly well-to-do."

"That's always relative, isn't it? From my standpoint she was. She told me once she had an income of thirty thousand a year. She didn't need to work, but she pre-

16

ferred having an interesting job to being just a society girl. Anyhow, she wasn't successful as a debutante and Peg wasn't the kind to go on hanging on the vine. She didn't like being second-rate at anything."

"Thirty thousand a year. That sounds like a nice little windfall. Who inherits?"

"I have no idea. We never discussed it. Naturally."

This time there could be no doubt that the look the trooper gave her was frankly disbelieving. "Well," he pushed back his chair, "sorry to have brought you this bad news. I'll pick you up tomorrow at eleven at the bank."

"Why do the New York police want to see me?" she asked.

"As a formality they will want you to identify the body, of course, though the building manager has done that. There's no real question of her identity. The elevator operator saw the body and so did a caller. But they will have some questions. As a close friend, you would know more about her circle of intimates than anyone else."

"Intimates! But I thought you said it was a burglar who—killed her?"

"Do you know anyone of the name of Fullbright?"

Because she was completely unprepared for the question, there was nothing to read in Judy's expressive face but sheer surprise.

"I just wondered. That's the name of the guy who found her. He said he had met her this morning for the first time. He had a business appointment with her for this evening. The police wondered why he was so insistent on getting into the apartment. Well—good night, Miss Wilkins."

The last thing Judy expected was that she would be able to rest, but she fell into a heavy sleep almost as soon as she got into bed. According to her little travel clock with its illuminated dial, it was nearly two when she was awakened by the muffled sound of voices. Or rather a single voice that seemed to drone on and on mechanically. A radio? She got out of bed and went to look out of the window. There was a police car parked near the front door, its radio tuned low. Inside a tiny light moved in an arc and she realized it was a cigarette. After a time the driver got out, stretched, looked automatically up at her window, got back inside.

For some reason a police guard was being kept on her. Anger flared, to be replaced by fear, and finally a kind of relief. Suppose the person who had killed the red-haired woman and then had killed Peg was still looking for the briefcase. Suppose he made the inevitable link between Peg and her. Suppose he came here. He worked fast. Terribly fast. Not more than an hour could have passed between the death of the red-haired woman and Peg's murder. At least no one could get past this guard.

If I hadn't taken Peg's briefcase—if I hadn't agreed to exchange briefcases with the red-haired woman— if—if—if— The fruitless regrets and self-tormenting went on for a long time. Just as she began to slide down the dark tunnel of sleep, Judy found herself wondering, rather dimly but without alarm, why the police had set a guard at the cottage. They didn't know of any potential danger she might be in. They must, therefore, believe she might have had a hand in the murder of her roommate. That was why the young trooper had wanted to know at what time she had got home. But why—there was an idea at the corner of her mind, but it slipped out of sight and she slept.

When she was awakened by the sound of her alarm, it was with a clear memory of everything that had happened the day before. This morning, she had expected, was going to be painful, because it would mean the relinquishing of the only home, the only belongings, the only roots, she had ever known. But now none of that mattered. It was submerged in the horror of Peg's murder.

She was going to New York to talk to the police about Peg. If the person who had killed her for the briefcase had not known before of Judy's existence, he would now. There would probably be something in the news about her. She would have to be careful, terribly careful, about what she said. And caution, as she was well aware, had never been her strong point. If it had been, she would not be in danger now, and Peg would not be—where she was. But how was she to throw the killer off the track unless she made a public statement about the briefcase, swore that she had lost it, and that she had never looked at its contents?

Her dress was the tailored white silk, a sleeveless sheath with a white matching coat which she had worn the day before. It had, Judy remembered with a pang, been a birthday present from Peg. Being a gift from Peg, it was exquisitely and cunningly cut so that it did full justice to the figure that was a shade too rounded for a high-fashion model.

When she had drunk a couple of cups of black coffee, she went out to say good morning to a trooper who was waiting in his car. It was not the same man she had talked with the night before, but she saw the same expression of surprise on his face that she had detected on the other man's. At least she did not look like a murderer. Murderess?

The trooper fell in behind her and trailed her to the bank. There was, Judy noticed, another police car parked outside the bank, and the man of the night before was seated at the wheel. The one who had followed her stopped to speak a few words and then drove on.

An hour later, after signing papers, more papers than there seemed to be any reason for, and receiving her check for three thousand eight hundred dollars, which she deposited, Judy shook hands with the new owners of her cottage, turned over keys, and went out to her car. She hesitated for a moment and then walked up to the police car.

"I planned to leave the Renault with a dealer here in town to sell for me. Would that be all right? I mean do you mind driving me in to New York or is there a law against it or something?"

"Of course." He followed her to the dealer's, where again she turned over papers and relinquished keys.

The trooper was standing beside his car, and he helped her into the seat beside him. There was a silence that threatened to become awkward. Then he said, "I hope you had a good rest last night after your shock."

"I did get some sleep. But it feels strange. Empty. I can't describe it."

"Empty?"

"Everything is gone. The only home I ever had. My car. Peg and the apartment. All the familiar things. There's just nothing left. Like a war or a fire or an epidemic or something that wipes things out."

"What are you planning to do now?" His voice was unexpectedly loud and she looked at him in surprise. "Sorry, I asked three times. Where were you?"

"Thinking about Peg. Did they hurt her much? I know how idiotic that sounds when they killed her, but somehow it matters a lot."

"From what I gathered over the telephone, she was hit on the head. The chances are that she never felt anything, never knew it was coming."

After that neither of them spoke until the police car drew up at the side of the road. The trooper nodded toward an unmarked car that had been parked. "New York will take over now." Seeing her expression, he smiled suddenly. "It will be all right, Miss Wilkins."

"Thank you."

The man in the New York car looked surprised when he saw her, like the others. He was courteous, helped her into the car, and aside from a few cautious glances did not pay any more attention to her until he drew up at a curb on lower Manhattan.

Judy looked around in surprise. "Where—?"

"The morgue," he told her briefly, and turned her over to the plainclothes man who was waiting.

The latter introduced himself as Lieutenant Krill. He was in his late thirties, with a round ruddy face that would remain youthful until he was sixty, and a cheerful manner. He gave her the surprised look to which she was becoming accustomed, but not reconciled, and escorted her into the morgue.

You could read about it forever, but it didn't help, it didn't prepare you for the moment when the sheet was drawn down from Peg's face. Apparently the lieutenant was accustomed to this moment because his hand tightened on her arm. But after the first uncontrollable start of horror, of rejection, as though this thing could be denied, could be made to go away, Judy was quiet, paler than usual, the freckles prominent on her face.

Yes, she said in a voice she did not recognize as her own, that was Margaret Morrison. She did not faint or lose consciousness, but the next ten minutes or so were blank for the rest of her life. She was aware of nothing until she was seated in the bleak-looking office across the table from Lieutenant Krill. There was a policeman in uniform sitting nearby with a notebook on his knee, and another policeman brought in a medium sort of young man, medium height and medium coloring and blunt features. For a moment Judy glanced at him and away again without interest. He was merely part of the general nightmare.

Lieutenant Krill looked at the policeman who had

accompanied the nondescript man and dismissed him. "All right, that's all. Oh, you had better send up coffee, coffee for four, and—Miss Wilkins, did you eat breakfast?"

It was a moment before his words made sense. She tried to remember. "I don't think so. Oh, no, I couldn't."

"Get some Danish pastries while you are at it," the lieutenant said.

"Thank you. That's very kind, but I'm not at all hungry. Just—stunned. Unbelieving, I guess."

"Of course."

The lieutenant was bland, so bland that Judy was instinctively on guard. She was aware, too, that the nondescript man had turned swiftly when he heard her name.

"Miss Wilkins," the lieutenant said, "this is Mr. Fullbright."

"I'm sorry, Miss Wilkins," the nondescript man said, "awfully sorry about your friend. I'm the one who found her." For some reason he felt that she needed to have the script written for her.

"You—how horrible for you, Mr.—"

"Fullbright. Jonathan Fullbright." His face didn't show much expression, but his eyes congratulated her on picking up her cue.

"How did it happen?" she asked.

"I have a commission to do some articles for *New Trends*. They require a lot of research, and the editor offered to have Miss Morrison help me with it. He said she was tops."

"Yes, she—" All of a sudden Judy realized that she was on the verge of breaking down. In place of the Peg she knew so well, slim, arrogant, exquisitely groomed, her expression sardonic, there was the face from which all expression had been wiped, the hair matted with blood, the— She clenched her teeth, shook her head as though to drive away the intolerable.

"I was to call her at six yesterday at her apartment after she had interviewed the Mayor and we were to spend the evening going over the material she had picked up and deciding whom to see next and what lines would be most effective to explore."

It was apparent that he had told this story more than once. He had telephoned the apartment several times and left messages. Finally, wondering whether anything could possibly be wrong, he had gone to the apartment himself and persuaded the elevator man to admit him.

Judy listened, her heart sinking. She wondered whether the story sounded as improbable to the impassive lieutenant as it did to her. Apparently the Fullbright man was going to shield her as long as he could. He wasn't going to volunteer the fact that she had been the one to worry about Peg, to worry for fear something had happened to her. And then she found herself gaping at him, aware that she must be staring like an owl. How did she know that any of his story was true? How did she know that he had not been the one who killed Peg, and that he was trying now to prevent her from mentioning the briefcase?

Something of that swift suspicion must have appeared on her face, because she realized that the lieutenant's gaze had become more intent.

"What—did you find?" she asked at length.

For the first time Krill checked Fullbright's story. "I'd like to have you both accompany me to the apartment," he said smoothly. "It's always easier to get the picture when you are on the spot, isn't it?"

"Yes, I—anyhow," Judy said blankly, "there's no place else for me to go, is there?"

"I don't know," the lieutenant said pleasantly. "Isn't there? What about your family?"

"I don't have anyone since my father died six months ago."

"Or Miss Morrison's family?"

Judy shook her head again.

"I think you told the Connecticut State Police there is a cousin, 'Maxwell something.' "

23

"I don't know his last name. All I know is that Peg didn't like him much."

"Why?"

"She never told me. If she had any special reason, she wouldn't have said so. Peg wasn't vindictive. She never loaded her dice against people by the way she spoke of them."

"I take it this cousin wasn't likely to be her heir."

"I suppose not."

"You don't know anything about Miss Morrison's will?"

"No, the man in Connecticut asked me that. She never mentioned it. There's no reason why she should, you know."

"There was a reason." Lieutenant Krill spoke softly. "We found her will in a drawer of her desk in the apartment last night. You're sure you never saw it?"

"But I wouldn't look through Peg's desk." Judy was more puzzled than annoyed. "I have one of my own."

"We noticed that. But we thought, perhaps, seeing that you are concerned—"

Margaret Morrison, he told her, had left her entire estate to her friend Judith Wilkins.

3

Somewhere a typewriter clattered, which was not a sound Judy would normally have associated with a police station. Someone was answering a telephone. Someone else was calling Car Eighteen persistently. But in the office where Judy faced the lieutenant there was no sound at all.

In spite of the fact that she had started the morning by warning herself to guard her tongue, she said, as usual, the first thing that came into her mind.

"So that's why there was a state trooper outside my cottage all night. I couldn't understand it. I thought I was being protected, not suspected."

The Fullbright man did not move; there was no discernible expression on his face, but she was aware that he was willing her not to speak. Friend or foe? She didn't even know that.

"I didn't kill Peg, Lieutenant," she said steadily.

"My dear young woman," the lieutenant protested, "You haven't been accused."

"I know. Just watched. In case. But I didn't."

Krill smiled at her with a considerable display of teeth. The smile on the face of the tiger. "We don't make mistakes like that," he said, still beaming. A tiger? He was positively fatherly. The more benevolent he appeared, the more he frightened Judy. "Let's just run over the times again."

"Times?"

When had she left the apartment? About ten in the morning. Why? She was job-hunting. Any luck? None at all. Was she in need of money? Not now, because

25

she had just sold her cottage. But Miss Morrison had provided her with a room in her apartment? She had paid the rent? And supplied the food? And—let's say incidentals? Yes, Judy replied readily, Peg had paid for everything.

When had Judy returned to the apartment from her disappointing day? She hadn't, Judy said, been disappointed. She hadn't expected to find a job she liked at once. And she had not returned to the apartment at all because she had to attend the closing of the sale of her house this morning. She had gone to Danbury? Yes. By bus? What time had she got there? Had she stayed at the house all evening?

"I got home about seven-thirty. Then I remembered that I had cleared out the shelves and the refrigerator when I closed the house, so I had to go back to Danbury to get some food."

Had she seen anyone in Danbury who would remember her? Talked to anyone on the telephone? Again there was that curious tension in the office. Judy could almost feel the Fullbright man's hand covering her mouth. She shook her head.

Lieutenant Krill's fingers tapped on the desk. He sat looking at Judy. A policeman came in with containers of coffee and pieces of Danish pastry, which Krill distributed. At last, having finished his coffee, he looked around and pushed back his chair.

"We'll go up to your apartment." He corrected himself without emphasis, and yet the emphasis was implied, "Miss Morrison's apartment. Just a moment, while I leave a few messages."

He went out and the policeman who had been taking shorthand notes followed him. The door to the hall had been left open. Fullbright moved then. Watching the doorway, he opened the newspaper he was holding and put it before her.

"There's a story about your friend inside. Nothing you don't know." His voice was low, cautious, his eyes on the doorway. "But the woman on the subway —they've identified her. Some reporter made a routine check at the morgue and remembered her, though she had changed a lot. She was an old actress on the skids. Dolores Costanza."

"An actress! I should have known because she articulated so beautifully. Trained." Judy looked down at the picture.

FORMER ACTRESS DIES ON
SUBWAY TRACKS

Dolores Costanza, once a movie star, jumped or fell to her death during the five o'clock rush on the Broadway express tracks at Forty-second Street.

There was no time to read the rest of the story. The picture seemed to bear little resemblance to the haggard redhead of the subway car. This woman had the over-made-up eyes of a past generation, the exotic dress of an old-time siren, and spectacular dangling diamond earrings—at least, in the photograph, they looked like real diamonds.

"Ever see her before?"

Judy shook her head. "It must be the same woman, but she didn't look much like that when she spoke to me."

Fullbright folded the paper, tucked it under his arm, and went to the window where he lighted a cigarette. "I'm awfully sorry about your friend," he said clearly. "This must be a terrible shock to you."

"I—yes, it is. It's hard to associate Peg with violence of any kind. She couldn't even endure emotional scenes. She was—a kind of understated person."

Lieutenant Krill was back again, attended by his faithful assistant. "Shall we go?" he asked as cheerfully as though he were suggesting a gay sort of outing.

To Judy's relief the trip was made in an unmarked police car. Though the story of Peg's murder was probably known to everyone in the apartment building, perhaps to everyone on the block, it was pleasanter not to arrive under obvious police escort.

The foyer was unobtrusive in its elegance, its unstressed luxury. A quiet woman looked up from the switchboard at one side. The elevator man stared at Judy in wide-eyed interest and embarrassment.

"Miss Wilkins!" he exclaimed, when the four of them had entered the elevator. "Gosh, you could of knocked me over when I saw—"

"Yes, I know. But how did anyone get in? That's what I can't understand."

"Well—" He looked at Fullbright and hesitated.

"It's all right," Fullbright told him. "The police know I was here and that you admitted me. After all, I was the one who called them."

"Well," the elevator man said uneasily, "I brought Miss Morrison up about five. She seemed—you know how she was." He appealed to Judy. "Everyone else who came in yesterday afternoon said something about the weather and grouched about the heat, and she just said in her brisk sort of way, 'I hear you get your vacation next week, Jake,' and she gimme a twenty-dollar bill and said I was to buy myself a drink. Some drink! And then she didn't even let me say thank you. She never did. She just said, in a hurry like, 'And if you have any sense, you'll go to the North Pole.' And she laughed and went to her own door."

"Do you think," Judy asked, "someone could have been waiting there?"

Jake shook his head. "Nope. I got out of the elevator to open the hall windows at either end of the corridor and get a breeze—there's no fire escapes near them windows," he told the detective hastily, "and I saw Miss Morrison unlock her door and go down the hall to turn on the air conditioning. She had some packages in her arms and she didn't even wait to put them down. I could see all through the apartment, the bedroom doors and the kitchen door, all open. There wasn't anyone there. And the only other person who asked for her was this guy here. He called up a couple of times, according to Hazel at the switchboard, and he left messages. Then he came around—maybe seven-thirty."

"And you let him in?"

"Well, I knew I'd brought Miss Morrison up, see? And she hadn't gone down again. So I was worried when she didn't answer the telephone. I unlocked the door for this guy here and went in with him. She was," he swallowed, "lying right there with her head all—"

"For God's sake!" Fullbright protested, although the lieutenant had nothing to say. He was watching Judy, who was looking at the stain on the cream-colored carpet, Judy, who was beginning to sway.

The elevator operator gulped, looked at the lieutenant for permission to leave, muttered something about being sorry, and went back to his cage.

The apartment had been furnished by Peg. There was the cream carpet that seemed to be about six inches thick, chairs upholstered in straw satin, and a spectacular curved red velvet couch. There was a small dining room paneled in dark oak, two bedrooms with baths, Peg's furnished with a four-poster bed whose hangings had been copied from those on Napoleon's; Judy's with a trim studio couch; a small modern kitchen, though nearly all the meals were sent up by the excellent restaurant next door. The building provided maid service.

Judy had already become accustomed to the beauty and luxury of the apartment. What she noticed now, when she could drag her eyes away from the stain on the carpet, was that the exquisite neatness with which Peg always surrounded herself was gone. The place had been ransacked.

"It's just chaos," she said helplessly.

"But selective. The desks weren't touched, for one thing, nor the smaller drawers in the bathrooms and bedrooms. Someone was looking for something fairly large—or giving the impression of looking for something." The lieutenant did not glance at Judy as he spoke. He didn't need to. His voice had the effect of a

29

pointed finger. She was poor and she inherited; therefore she had killed Peg. And her alibi was no good. Who would remember that she had been on that crowded bus for Danbury between five and six when Peg must have been killed? She herself could not remember a single face; she had not even noticed whether the passenger in the seat beside her was a man or a woman.

"I suppose," Krill said, "you are the only person who could tell whether anything was stolen. If you'd —just look around." He sat down comfortably on the big couch and lighted a cigarette.

Judy walked carefully around the stain on the carpet and opened Peg's desk, which, like everything of Peg's, was orderly. She looked at the receipted bills, the small pile of unanswered mail, a neat file of expenses and insurance policies and stocks for her tax records, checkbooks, savings bankbooks. She said hopelessly, "I've never looked in Peg's desk before. I don't know whether everything is here or not."

"As I told you, we found her will and got in touch with her lawyer. She seems to have been a very methodical young lady. Everything listed down."

Judy got up to turn on the air conditioning, pushed back the fluffy light hair that was beginning to curl tightly over her damp forehead, and slipped off the white silk coat. It was going to be another breathless, sweltering day. Only Peg in that chilled— Stop it! You can't think about that.

The search of her own bedroom required only minutes. She looked at her scanty wardrobe, through the contents of overturned dresser drawers, and shook her head. Everything had been thrown around, but nothing was missing.

The same chaos existed in Peg's room, clothes pushed aside in the closet, the dresser drawers dumped on the floor, bedding pulled back to reveal the mattress.

"I don't know," Judy said at last. "Peg had a lot of clothes, but I don't see why anyone would kill her to take them. And there's nothing else anyone would want." Remembering what Peg had said about lying, she kept her eyes down. Oh, Peg, she told her silently, I'm learning. Oh, Peg, if I had only done as you told me!

"I take it, then," Lieutenant Krill said at last, "you don't know of anything that has been stolen."

She shook her head.

"We'll be in touch. Don't go away without informing us. Anyhow, you'll want to arrange for the funeral, of course, as you seem to be the closest to her of anyone."

"Oh, yes, of course."

"We'll let you know when the body can be released." Krill caught the eye of the policeman who had accompanied him.

Jonathan Fullbright was still standing at the window in the living room where he had been ever since he entered the apartment. He was aware that Krill was waiting for him to make a move.

"You haven't had anything to eat, have you, Miss Wilkins?" Fullbright said. "I noticed that you didn't touch the pastry."

"No, I couldn't swallow."

"Suppose you let me get you some coffee. Will they send it up from the restaurant?"

"Yes, but that isn't necessary. There are things in the kitchen."

"Then I'll take care of it. I'm used to doing my own cooking."

The lieutenant hesitated and Judy had a curious feeling that he did not like the idea of leaving them together. Then he went out.

Fullbright waited until he heard the elevator door close and then he pushed her gently into a chair. "All right, take it easy. I'll bring you some coffee."

She sat quite still, fighting against the horrifying memory of Peg with the battered head, Peg lying so still in that cold room. There was no doubt at all in her mind that Lieutenant Krill believed she had staged the upheaval in the apartment and killed her roommate for her money.

She had almost forgotten Fullbright's existence when he brought a tray and set it on a small table beside her. There was not only a pot of coffee, but a scrambled egg on toast, and a half grapefruit carefully scooped out.

"Go ahead and eat. You are going to need it, you know. We'll talk later."

He waited patiently until she had eaten all the food and had drunk two cups of coffee. Then she sat back and for the first time really noticed him. There was nothing particularly striking about his appearance at first glance, certainly not a man whom women would turn to stare at on the street. Then she realized that, in an unstressed sort of way, he was a good-looking man. Compact of body, quiet of manner and of dress, his more arresting qualities were hard to define. But anyone, she thought, would be aware that Jonathan Fullbright was pleasantly at home in his world, self-confident without being offensive about it, and self-sufficient without disregarding others.

"Now then," he said, "I think you had better tell me about it. I couldn't make much out of that telephone conversation last night except that you were in a spot because of some briefcase, and that the death of your roommate and of the actress on the subway are tied up in some way. You sounded nearly frantic. That's why, after seeing what had happened to Miss Morrison, I realized that someone is playing for keeps, and I thought it might not be smart to mention the briefcase. It might give someone a bright idea, or set you up as target Number Three." He added rather dubiously, "I hope I was right."

"I hope you were," Judy said dully, "but he seems to kill first anyhow, doesn't he? That poor frightened woman on the subway and then Peg. He just killed them without even trying to make sure they had the right briefcase. And now he'll know I am Peg's roommate and that the briefcase wasn't in the apartment, so he'll be after me. And there's no place to hide, is there, when you don't know from whom you are hiding?"

"Anyone," he said lightly, "who can manage a dative case in these circumstances is a woman after my own heart." He added, the laughter gone from his voice, "Hadn't you better tell me what this is all about?"

"I don't know what it's all about," Judy said. She told him of her curious conversation with the terrified red-haired woman on the subway, and how she had agreed to the exchange of briefcases. "And the one I had was Peg's, with her name and address in it. So when the woman's body was found and wasn't identified, I knew someone had taken the briefcase. And then when Peg—"

"You aren't going to faint or be sick or anything, are you?" he asked anxiously.

She shook her head, though she wasn't at all sure.

"But even suppose someone got your roommate's briefcase when the woman was pushed onto the express tracks, and found the name and address, how would he know which apartment she had? Apparently no one asked for her at the switchboard. Except me, of course."

Judy went to Peg's desk, opened a drawer and pulled out a small package of printed name and address slips with adhesive on the back. "I noticed these when I was searching the desk for the lieutenant."

He saw the name Margaret Morrison, the street address, the apartment number. "So that's that, if he didn't mind walking up fourteen flights of stairs. But he'd still be seen entering the building and, in a place like this, he would certainly be challenged."

"He could have taken the freight elevator from the basement. All he would have had to do would be to watch and make sure the superintendent wasn't in sight. And in a building this size, with deliveries all the time, and the usual cuts in service that most buildings seem to have now, there isn't someone on duty in the basement twenty-four hours a day or even twelve hours."

"So it was easy enough to find the apartment. But would Miss Morrison be likely to admit a stranger, someone who had not been announced?"

Judy nodded and swallowed hard. "She would think I had come back for some reason. I've already lost two keys. She'd have opened the door, thinking it was me."

"Steady there," he said quietly. "You are too intelligent to believe you are responsible for her death. It just isn't true, you know. Personally, I'll bet that your roommate would have done the same thing."

"You mean she would have exchanged briefcases to help that frightened woman?"

"Unless she was cautious beyond reason—and beyond pity."

"Thank God for that!" Judy released her breath in a long sigh of relief.

"Now then," he said, sounding very practical, "what did you do with the woman's briefcase?"

"As soon as you had talked to me the second time and told me about Peg, I got in the car and drove back to Danbury. I stuck the briefcase in the back of the first open truck I saw and drove away. Nobody noticed me. I just— All I wanted was to get rid of the thing."

"It seemed like a good idea at the time," Fullbright admitted.

"And the woman herself told me that if she didn't get away, I was to do as I saw fit. It wouldn't matter then, she said."

"And now?"

Judy's eyes were direct and frankly terrified. "There's no use fooling myself, is there? Now I'm between the devil and the deep blue sea. Don't you think I know the position I'm in? I haven't got the briefcase, I don't know where it is, I don't know what was in it. I don't even know why it could be dangerous enough to be worth killing two women for. I don't know how to protect myself because I don't know what I'm to be protected against. And if I can't produce that briefcase, the chances are that the police are going to arrest me for Peg's murder because she left everything to me and there isn't anyone else with a motive for killing her, and I haven't got an alibi that's worth two cents."

4

Fullbright cleared away the dishes, working with a minimum of noise and fuss, and came back to offer her a cigarette. She shook her head.

"What about this cousin of Miss Morrison?"

"Maxwell? Oh, that's absurd. Peg didn't like him much; he's an actor and rather precious and conceited, and just not her type. But as far as I know, he is fairly successful; certainly he is solvent, and he is no more addicted to violence than I am."

"An actor?" Fullbright said alertly. "Do you think there is any possible tie-in between him and the dead actress?"

"I've only met him twice, and that was months ago. I haven't any idea whom he knew. But the woman looked—I doubt if she had had a part in a long time. She looked as though she were down on her luck; she was shabby, and she needed a face-lifting job, and she had home-dyed hair. No, I can't imagine her getting a job on television, and that is where Maxwell works."

"Then he ought to be easy to check on. Apparently nothing was stolen, though this was the only apartment in the building to be entered. Miss Morrison was at home, which meant the intruder knew he'd be taking an unnecessary chance, unless it was his only chance. As for motive—all right, all right, don't look like that! I don't think you did it. I'm just thinking out loud. So we are left with the people who want the briefcase. But how in hell we are to find out who they are, I can't imagine."

"I wish I'd kept it!" Judy wailed. "I must have panicked. In fact, I know I panicked. All I could think of was that I wanted to get rid of the thing, as though I were carrying plague germs around with me. But without it I'll have the police on my neck. They will never believe my story unless I can produce the damned thing. Why should they? And once my association with Peg gets into the news—and that may be right now, for all I know—I'll have someone else on my trail and I don't know who he is."

"So," Fullbright said, "that leaves us with just two possibilities: we've got to find that briefcase and discover what danger it represents, draw its fangs, in a manner of speaking, or—"

"But I tell you I don't know where it is."

"We can but try."

"We?"

"I'm in this," he said.

"Why?"

For a moment he seemed rather at a loss. "Well," he said at last, "you're in a spot and I'm the one who gave you the bad advice about getting rid of the briefcase."

"If it weren't for that," Judy admitted candidly, "I'd be wondering about you."

Unexpectedly he chuckled. "Well, yes, I can see your point. But, if it's any satisfaction to you, the police have already checked on me, not only with *New Trends,* where an editor confirmed my arrangement with Miss Morrison and gave me a nice build-up, but they've been in touch with my literary agent and know that I am solvent and reasonably respectable. Come on, let's get cracking."

"I don't know what you want to do."

"I have a car garaged on Ninety-sixth Street. Let's pick it up and go in search of the briefcase."

"That is just plain silly."

"Then, if we can't find it, we'll do the next best thing: try to trace back and find out what friends and enemies this Dolores Costanza had. That should give us some sort of lead."

"But how in the world can we do that?"

"Don't raise so many difficulties, my child. I don't know how. The how will undoubtedly suggest itself later. Come on."

II

They had nearly reached the door when the telephone rang.

"Miss Wilkins?"

"This is Miss Wilkins."

"I've just heard of the tragic death of your roommate, Margaret Morrison. I want to tell you how very sorry I am."

"I—thank you."

"Margaret and I are very dear old friends and just recently, as she has probably told you, we've been engaged on a research job for *New Trends*. I hate to disturb you at a tragic time like this, and if it weren't for a deadline, I wouldn't. The thing is I'm wondering if she turned over to you a briefcase containing the material we've been working on."

"Why—"

"You've seen the briefcase?"

"Well, yes, but—"

"Fine. I'll have someone there to pick it up in ten minutes." The man at the other end of the line hung up before Judy could make any further comment.

Fullbright reached her in three long strides. "What is wrong?"

"That was him. He." Judy repeated the conversation. "No one ever called Peg Margaret in all her life. And she wasn't working on another project. She had just finished one. And he is sending someone for the briefcase right away."

Ten minutes later the house telephone shrilled. "A messenger for you, Miss Wilkins," the woman at the switchboard said. "Shall I send him up?"

Beside Judy, Fullbright nodded emphatically.

"All right." She was standing rigid with fear when the two-toned chimes rang. She took a long breath and opened the door.

"I'm from *New Trends,*" the boy said. "I was sent to collect a briefcase."

"Come off it." Fullbright's hand jingled coins suggestively in his pocket. "Who really sent you?"

The boy grinned guilelessly, undisturbed that his story was not accepted. "I don't know. A gent down the street. In the drugstore. He gave me two bucks to collect it."

Fullbright gave him a dollar. "Tell him that Miss Wilkins has already sent it to *New Trends.* Hey, wait! On second thought, I'll go along and tell him myself."

Twenty minutes later Fullbright returned, having himself carefully announced first. He shook his head in disgust when Judy opened the door for him. "There was a guy standing in front of the drugstore. When he saw that the kid was empty-handed, he took off like a jet. I was right behind the messenger. The kid tried to point him out, but he was moving too fast. I just caught a glimpse of a gray coat."

"You did your best," Judy consoled him.

"I goofed again, and this time I goofed in a big way because now it is clear to him that you know the importance of the briefcase and lied about it."

"So what do we do?"

"Follow the original plan," Fullbright said promptly, "and try to locate the truck. If we draw a blank——"

"We will," she said glumly. "Do you know how many trucks there are in the United States? And the whole point is that they go places? And I didn't even take a good look at it."

"Then we'll try the hard way by sifting the background of Dolores Costanza."

"Looking for what?"

"God knows. But I can tell you this: it's something big or two women wouldn't have been killed to get possession of the briefcase. We'll know it when we find it."

They took a circuitous route to the Ninety-sixth Street garage, using a crosstown bus, a subway, and a taxi.

"Is all this really necessary?" Judy asked when, after a careful look up and down the street, Fullbright rushed her across the sidewalk from the taxi and into the garage. "I feel ridiculous with all this dodging about, playing cloak and dagger."

"I rather enjoy it myself," Fullbright admitted. "It adds savor to an otherwise routine trip." He spoke lightly, but Judy noticed that he tried to leave the garage at a moment when a red light at the corner held up oncoming traffic.

"Do you really think someone will try to follow us?"

"I have no idea," he said shortly. Then, as he seemed to be engrossed in his own thoughts and not inclined to talk, Judy opened his newspaper. Once more she looked at the old picture of the red-haired woman who had died on the subway tracks, the woman who had involved Peg and herself and the man Fullbright in a fantastic series of events.

A reporter with a long memory had made a routine check of the morgue, seen the woman, and identified her. Dolores Costanza, born Doris Curtis in Gary, Indiana, in 1910, was an American phenomenon, a girl who had attained stardom in the movies without learning how to act. She had been the sex symbol of her day, glamorous rather than popular, but when she became involved in some highly publicized scandals, her box-office appeal began to dwindle and she started to drink heavily.

Her last starring picture had been in 1953. Since then she had had a few supporting roles, had appeared occasionally on the straw-hat circuit, and more recently had done some television commercials, pointing out the advantages of various detergents, mouthwashes, and floor polishes. She was the woman who was perpetually astounded by the miracles worked by these products.

At the time of her death she occupied a furnished

room in a "family hotel" in the West Forties in the theatrical district and, according to the manager of the building, her rent was several months in arrears, though she had promised that she would be able to pay it in a few days as she expected a "windfall."

"About all you can make out of that story," Fullbright commented, "is that she was on the skids."

"She was terrified," Judy told him. "No one could have mistaken that." She turned pages, looking for the story about Peg.

HOUSEBREAKER SLAYS
WOMAN TENANT

Margaret Morrison, 28, of 740 East 55th Street, was found dead last evening by Jonathan Fullbright when he called to discuss an article on which they were collaborating for *New Trends.* Alarmed because Miss Morrison failed to answer her telephone, the elevator man, who had taken her to her apartment at five o'clock, admitted Fullbright at seven-thirty.

Miss Morrison had been struck on the head, apparently by a burglar who had ransacked the apartment. The time of her death was estimated as between five-thirty and six o'clock. For two years she had been a researcher for *New Trends,* after making her debut in 1962 and spending several years at the Sorbonne in Paris. No immediate family has been found.

Miss Morrison had been assigned to work with Jonathan Fullbright on a series of articles on city government in preparation for which she interviewed the Mayor yesterday afternoon. According to his secretary she left his office at four-thirty.

Mr. Fullbright, author of the best-selling *Such Men Are Dangerous* and articles on practical politics that have appeared in most of the leading periodicals, is also a popular lecturer on the participation of the individual in government.

Judy looked at Fullbright in some surprise. Apparently he was much more distinguished and important than she had realized. She wondered why he felt it incumbent on himself to devote valuable time to help her unravel the puzzle in which she was involved, and with which he was only tangentially concerned. Nevertheless, she was aware of an enormous feeling of relief. She had never been accustomed to the luxury of having someone take the responsibility for her, and the feeling was so pleasant that she warned herself that it could not last, she must not expect it to last.

"So far," she said, "there's no mention of me. I wonder how that man knew I was Peg's roommate."

"When the paper went to press, you hadn't yet appeared on the scene." Fullbright leaned forward to switch on his radio, waited while an announcer rattled through the day's catastrophes and pointed out with relish that the temperature would probably reach a new high. There was, he went on cheerfully, no relief in sight.

"Judith Wilkins," and she stiffened, "roommate of Margaret Morrison, found dead last evening in her luxury apartment on the East Side, was brought back from Connecticut and questioned by the police this morning. Miss Wilkins has been named Miss Morrison's heir."

Fullbright shut off the radio. "I'd like to get my hands on that so-and-so. He's just asking for a law suit to be brought against him. And a broken jaw."

"If," Judy said, "I were hearing that story about a stranger, I would assume that this roommate was hard up and killed Peg because she wanted to inherit her money. Brought back by the police for questioning. You had better drop out of the picture right now, Mr. Fullbright."

"The name is Jon," he said absently.

"I mean it," she told him. "I'm going to be the untouchable of Fifty-fifth Street." When he made no immediate disclaimer, she added, "There's no reason why you should be tarred with the same brush."

"That's a mixed metaphor," he pointed out. "Anyhow, I regard this as good publicity."

"If that newspaper article is reliable, you don't need any publicity you can't provide for yourself."

"I am not altruistic," he said earnestly, as though clearing himself of some shameful charge. "I'm interested. Actually I am seething with curiosity. Now then," as they entered Danbury, "let's see how good you are at finding your way."

She directed him quickly toward the residential streets, then indicated turns more slowly. "I'm just not sure. I tell you I wasn't really looking. All I had in mind was finding something, maybe a garbage can, anything, and just getting rid of that accursed briefcase."

He didn't seem disturbed. It would, she was beginning to realize, take quite a lot to disturb him. "You saw more than you realized you did. One always does. Stop panicking and try to remember. It was evening, of course, and the light was different, the traffic was different. Were there many cars parked on the block?"

"No, nothing but the truck. I'm sure of that."

"You didn't notice anything about the truck? Color? Shape? Name?"

She shook her head. "It was big," she said unhelpfully.

"What kind of truck would be making deliveries after seven in the evening? An oil truck?"

"Not in midsummer. Anyhow, the back was open, don't you remember? That's why I was able to put the briefcase inside."

"Deliveries from a grocer?" he suggested.

"Much too big for that. Anyhow——" And then the picture came back to her clearly. "The house was wide open, and there were lights all over the place, and there were boxes and crates in the front hall."

"A moving van?"

"It must have been! Oh, Jon! I never thought we'd find out so easily."

"Don't go overboard," he warned her. "We aren't there yet. Now then, what kind of neighborhood was it? Old houses, new houses, well-kept, rundown?"

"Old houses. Not affluent, but not down-at-heel. And I hadn't gone far, perhaps two or three blocks."

"All right. Any idea whether you turned right or left?"

"No. Yes! Yes, I do. I turned left. There was a little boy on a bicycle turning right at the corner and I didn't want him to remember me, so I turned left."

He was going more slowly now. "That's it!" she cried. She added in a tone of astonishment, "You know, I never thought we'd really find it."

5

The house was empty, with a FOR SALE sign and the address of a real estate agent in the front yard, which had turned brown with the heat. Fullbright, who did not appear to share Judy's consternation—after all, as he pointed out, a moving van indicated that people were moving—suggested that they try the real estate office first.

There was no air conditioning in the office on Main Street, only a fan that seemed to move around the hot air rather than cool it. A rather stout woman wielding a ragged palm-leaf fan looked up at them as they came in, her shrewd eyes attempting to estimate their probable financial status. Apparently she took them for bride and groom.

She waved them to chairs. "What can I do for you? I have some lovely properties right now. You couldn't have chosen a better time." She beamed at Judy. "What do you have in mind, Mrs.—uh—"

"It's Miss Wilkins." To her annoyance Judy found herself blushing.

"We aren't in the market for a house," Fullbright said, "but we'd like some information about one you have for sale." He gave the address.

"Well, what information?" She was busy turning over cards. "The fabric is absolutely sound. A little decoration, of course—"

"Who are the owners?" he asked.

She referred to the card file. "It's one of the properties owned by an insurance company. Now let's see—"

"Then the last people who were living there—"

"Mr. William Pitten. The Pittens were just renting. He had a small business in New York and sold out. He and his wife—elderly, you know, not in good health—wanted to live in a quieter place. They were just sort of trying out Danbury. But then—nothing about the house had anything to do with it—the poor man got this condition, whatever it was, and pneumonia, and the doctor said he had to go out West where it would be dry, Arizona or New Mexico. They left a couple of weeks ago. Made quite a fuss about paying the rent, but they had taken a year's lease and we agreed to refund if anyone else moved in."

"They left a couple of weeks ago!" Judy exclaimed. "But the moving van was there yesterday." Again she had the curious feeling that Fullbright was ordering her to be silent.

The woman did not appear to be curious. "Well, they didn't have much stuff of their own; the house is mostly furnished, beds and chairs, electric stove and refrigerator, all that. They sent their personal stuff along with some other small loads because it would be cheaper than hiring a whole van for a few pieces."

"What is their new address?" Fullbright asked.

"Anything wrong with the Pittens?" The woman answered her own question, dismissing the idea. "Oh, there couldn't be."

"Not that we know of, but it is important to reach them. A legal matter." Fullbright let the idea drop.

"Well, I'm sure I don't know how you'll reach them right away. They were going to stop to visit their two daughters in the Middle West on their way, and I don't know the married names of the daughters or even what states they live in. Then they expected to stay at a motel in Phoenix while they looked around for a place. I suppose their stuff was to go into storage, but I don't know how long it would take to get there. With a number of loads, the van could be stopping all across the country. I was to advise the Pittens at General Delivery in Phoenix if I got any offers for the house and could refund some of the rent, but there aren't many people looking these days, what with the heat and all."

When they reached the street, Judy said, "Well, that's a dead end, if there ever was one."

" 'Courage, he said, and pointed to the land.' "

This poetic outburst did nothing to raise her spirits. "We are completely and beautifully stuck."

"We are nothing of the sort. Remember that if worst comes to worst we can always go to the police and put them on the track of the moving van and the brief-case. They would have ways of locating that van within hours."

"And if the briefcase was taken off with someone else's stuff or lost or—even if they found it, has it occurred to you that the police already suspect that I killed Peg and they may think I pushed Dolores Costanza off the subway platform as well?"

"The worst is not what necessarily happens. If there is no other way, we can go out to Arizona ourselves. But before looking for needles in haystacks, let's apply our powerful intellects to something more fruitful."

An hour later, after talking to the neighbors along the block where the William Pittens had lived, they had added nothing to their store of information. The couple had been elderly. He hadn't been in good health and people had seen little of them. Nice, you know, but sort of withdrawn. We'd have been glad to be neighborly but, you know how it is, if they'd rather be alone—

Mrs. Pitten had spoken of two married daughters. One lived in Chicago and the other somewhere in Ohio. The married name of one, someone said help-fully, was Smith. No one had paid any particular attention to the moving van or noticed what company owned it, or had even observed the color.

Back in the car, whose seat was scorching, Judy pushed her hair off her forehead, jerked her arm off the burning armrest.

"What we need," Fullbright said after a look at her, "is a nice cold drink in a nice cold bar."

"Women can't sit at a bar in Connecticut. It's against the law."

"What an obstructionist you are! There will be tables."

"And probably a juke box or a television set," she remarked.

"You would not," he informed her, "be my chosen companion on a desert island. This incessant gloom, this—"

"I keep seeing Peg. This really isn't hilariously funny."

His hand covered hers for a moment. "I know that. And I loathe people who try to be bright little souls and the life of the party. Forgive me."

He stopped to get cigarettes and, to her surprise, bought a television guide, which he dropped on her lap. "There's a cool place where we can get a drink down on the next block. I just asked."

"What's this for?"

"The guide? I thought you might try to find the elusive Maxwell something listed in it."

"As I remember him, there is nothing particularly elusive about Maxwell; he's just not—memorable. But I'll try." She was aware that Fullbright was trying to focus her attention on something constructive that would help her shut out the picture of Peg with her crushed head, and she was grateful, but she had already learned enough about him not to say so. For some reason Fullbright did not fancy the role of benefactor.

She looked through the afternoon programs. "I know he has one of those steady jobs in a story that goes on and on and apparently is very successful. I've never seen it myself. One of those things that are really gold mines without having any discernible advantage over any other program. I think he said it's on five afternoons a week. I know he was complaining because it didn't give him much scope, but it was as secure as such things can be. Like one of those long-lasting plays, *Life with Father,* where the children kept growing up and having to be replaced by younger ones until it ended with one of the original children playing the father. Except, as I remember Maxwell, he could probably play either part."

"And that," Fullbright commented, "is an extremely nasty comment."

"Maxwell's deepest grief is that the girl who plays his wife in this opus is featured and he isn't. I think— *Pot of Gold!* I'm pretty sure that's the one. It's listed as the Mavis Donnelly show."

The cocktail bar was dim and cool, with no customers at this early hour. There was a television screen. When they had ordered gin and tonic, Fullbright asked the waiter if he would mind switching on the *Pot of Gold* program. In some surprise the waiter agreed.

After watching the first fifteen minutes of the show, Fullbright could understand the surprise. Mavis Donnelly, the star of this program, played a bird-witted young wife who might have been a Grade B Dulcie, without the charm or the humor of the original. She seemed always headed for disaster, but some core of wisdom in her heart of gold led her to victory, followed by the amazement of her adoring but conservative husband, who was perpetually alarmed by her behavior. The husband was played by Maxwell—Fullbright had seen the name in small letters on the screen —Allington. Good God! What names these actors picked!

Maxwell, it seemed to Fullbright, was admirably cast. He had one of those perpetually youthful faces that would enable him to play juvenile roles until he was fifty. He wore a look of perpetual surprise, which was probably normal for him, the general effect of his unfathomable world. He spoke his lines with a deadly combination of boyish charm and determination to make them sound important that caricatured a part which already verged on caricature.

When, at the end of the first half of this breathless drama, some newcomers at the bar complained, Fullbright nodded to the waiter who, in relief, turned off the television set and substituted Music by Musak, to prevent the ultimate horror of peace and quiet in the room.

They drove slowly back to New York. There was a breeze now that lifted Judy's hair. Beside her, Fullbright was silent, his hands competent on the wheel. He was, she saw in relief, a reliable rather than a dashing driver.

"What's worrying you?" he asked at last.

"I should have cashed a check while I was in Danbury. I don't want to go back to the apartment. I can't bear to go back there."

"We'll think of something," he said.

"Look here," she protested, "you've done enough. You just—drop me off somewhere. I'll have to do my own thinking."

At a stop light he turned to smile at her. "Don't fuss so," he said gently. "Leave this to me. You can't drop me out of the picture now. Fascinating stories are always appearing in the news, haven't you noticed? And then they just fade out. I want to hear the end of this one."

That wasn't the truth. She was pretty sure that wasn't the truth. But it was, she admitted to herself, sheer heaven to be able to shift the responsibility to Jonathan Fullbright's capable shoulders. She did not ask herself why he was so willing to assume it.

"Actually, I don't even know what to do next," she admitted, wallowing with secret delight in her first excursion into feminine dependence.

"Let's pay a couple of calls and then have a really good dinner—you've barely eaten anything today—and after that we'll see."

"What calls?"

"First—by the way, did you keep that newspaper? —oh, good. I want to see Dolores Costanza's landlady."

"Dolores! You know I'd almost forgotten her. What with Peg and looking for the briefcase—"

"But Dolores and the briefcase are the core of the matter." When she had read aloud the address from the news story, he said, "We'll never be able to park near the theatrical district. Suppose I garage the car and we take a cab."

It wasn't until after he had put her in a cab and given the address in the West Forties to the driver, that Judy noticed Fullbright was not really relaxed at all. Under his air of quiet competence he was alert and tense.

"Why," she asked, "did you pick this particular cab?"

He grinned at her. "Because our tail garaged his car where I did, and so I waited until there wasn't another cab in sight."

"Our tail!"

He nodded. "Ever since we left your apartment this morning. I did everything I could think of to throw him off the scent, but he's good. He's very good."

"Why didn't you tell me?"

"You are carrying quite a load as it is. Anyhow, I'll bet our trip to the real estate office threw him off. I don't honestly see what he can make of that."

He helped Judy out of the car and looked in disparagement at the big building. The street was noisy. Farther east there had been theater signs. Then the street deteriorated. There were bars and delicatessens, what appeared to be strip joints, movies marked "Adults Only," signs indicating that ballet and singing and guitar were taught.

There was no doubt that Dolores Costanza had been in a bad way. The big lobby of the so-called "family hotel" was dirty and smoke-filled, with a couple of shabby chairs and a number of overflowing ashtrays. An elderly man, unshaven and red-eyed, dozed at the switchboard.

"We'd like to see the manager," Fullbright said, when he had nudged the man to arouse his attention.

The tired old eyes moved from one face to the other as though scenting trouble. "What for? You looking for rooms?" He didn't sound as though he thought it likely.

"We'd like to ask her about a former tenant."

"Yeah?"

"Miss Costanza."

"Oh, that one." News of Costanza's death did not appear to have aroused general grief. "If you're going to pay her back rent, Miz Collins will be glad to see you." He plugged in, spoke so low they could not hear what he said. "Take a seat."

Not liking the looks of the chairs, Judy and Fullbright remained standing. Now and then someone came through the revolving door from the street. Most of the tenants were in late middle age, and they all looked as though they were or had been actors who had never quite made the grade. They moved as though they were a little larger than life; their gestures were a little broader; their voices, as a rule, carried clearly. Judy remembered the red-haired woman's beautiful articulation.

The manager was tall and gaunt and stooped, with improbable red hair, thick make-up on cheeks that were mostly jowls, pouches under her eyes. She had no more chest than a scooped-out melon rind. She was probably seventy, and she looked as though nothing could either surprise or shock her any more, if she had ever been easily shocked.

She looked at the old man at the switchboard, who nodded toward them. "You friends of Dolores?"

There was no grief in her face but there was, quite unmistakably, fear. She seemed braced for trouble. At that moment Jon got his first inkling of the meaning of the briefcase.

"We'd like to talk to you about her," he said.

Judy looked at the woman in a kind of wonder, a mixture of pity and revulsion. And people talked about a mellow old age! This woman had not mellowed, she had simply hardened. And now she was afraid. Old and tired and afraid. And possibly dangerous as well. Like a maimed tiger who becomes a man-killer for survival.

Mrs. Collins shrugged in a fatalistic way. "Come on." She looked from one to the other. "But whatever you're after, you are too late." The elevator creaked and groaned its way to the fourth floor. The door she unlocked opened on a small dark room on a court. Apparently there was a cheap restaurant at the bottom of the shaft; the clatter of dishes and the smell of onions came into the room as she opened the filthy window and then turned on the light.

For a moment they stood in the doorway staring. "Yeah," Mrs. Collins said, looking from one to the other. "This is the way I found it when I brought the police up here."

Judy had a queer feeling that all this had happened to her before. The dresser drawers were upside down on the floor; a curtain strung on a rod across the wall to conceal a few shabby dresses had been ripped off; the bedding was pulled up to reveal the springs.

"This was Miss Costanza's room?" Fullbright asked.

"That's right. And there's nothing here, nothing the police could find. And I must say I don't know what anyone would be looking for. Dolores hasn't had a job for months. She pawned everything except the clothes she needed. Even the diamond earrings. She held on to those until the last. She hadn't paid me for two months. Not a penny. I don't know how she was eating."

"It was kind of you to let her stay on when she couldn't pay," Judy said.

Mrs. Collins gave her a quick look. "It wasn't for so long. And she had a windfall coming." There was a queer sound in her throat. "Some windfall that turned out to be! What you might call irony now. Anyhow, she was quite an old friend. And you know the saying, There's no business like show business. People in the profession stick together. I met her when she was a big name. Riding high. I played her mother in a pic-

53

ture, *Coasts of Darkness*. Maybe you remember. I came close to getting an award for a supporting role. Oh, well," as she looked from one blank face to the other, "it was a long time ago. And I haven't acted since then. Got married and quit. But I've still got some clippings in my scrapbook that would surprise you."

"What can you tell us about Miss Costanza?" Fullbright asked.

"What do you want to know for?"

He pulled out his billfold and withdrew a twenty-dollar bill. After a token hesitation she took it, folded it carefully, and put it in her pocket.

"Well, I hardly know what to tell you. She did mighty well for a time. Top of the heap. Box-office appeal, starring roles, money, jewelry, men. You name it, she had it. But she couldn't act. Not really. Then she got—oh, like involved in things and there was a lot of talk. And she just wasn't a box-office attraction any more. Real lemon she got to be. And from then on she was on the skids."

"Do you know any friends she had?"

Mrs. Collins gave a snort of laughter. "She wasn't the kind who made friends. She got where she was by clawing her way up. She didn't care who got hurt. And that, you might say, is what brought her down again."

"Married?"

"Once, but that goes back a long ways. I'd almost forgotten myself. Yeah, she was married when she was just a kid, like maybe eighteen."

"What was his name?"

"I don't know. They broke up a long time ago and later he remarried but she didn't. She wasn't the kind men usually marry."

"What caused the break-up?"

"What would you think? Another guy. It broke up his marriage, too."

"Anyone else you can think of she'd be involved with?"

"Men, you mean?" Mrs. Collins thought. "Well, I can't say Dolores was the confiding kind. Not with women. There was something. It had to do with those diamond earrings. The guy who gave them to her." She thought for a moment, shook her head. "Maybe it will come back to me."

Fullbright pulled out another twenty-dollar bill and handed it to her. "If you should think of anything else," he said.

"I know there was something wrong. Yes, I remember."

"I thought you might."

"He stole the money for those earrings and went to prison. She was scared out of her wits when he was released."

"Do you know who he was and approximately when this happened?"

"I can't think of anything." Mrs. Collins gave Fullbright a measuring look.

He reached for his card and handed it to her. "Just in case," he said.

"Well," Judy expelled a long breath when they had gone out onto the street, with its heat and smells and noise. "Well! I could believe that woman was capable of anything except taking in an old friend out of kindness."

"But Dolores was expecting a windfall," he said oddly. Then he smiled at her. "You're getting an education in the seamier facts of life faster than you expected." He tucked her hand under his arm. "One more call and then we'll have dinner."

"Now where?"

"Dear Maxwell, I think." He led her into a drugstore where he looked for a telephone directory. "Next stop the Village." He went out to hail a cruising taxi.

Maxwell occupied the smallest house Judy had ever seen. It was approached through the lobby of an apartment building on a side street in the Village. One went through the lobby and across a beaten-up piece of parched ground referred to as a garden, and there was the house. There were two rooms, a living room and kitchen combination on the first floor, and then, up a narrow flight of stairs, a bedroom and a small bath.

Maxwell was in the living room drinking a Bloody Mary and watching with disparagement his television competition. He was older and rather better-looking than he had appeared on the screen.

"Hello, Maxwell." This time she felt that it was up to her to take the lead. "I don't know whether you remember me. I'm a friend of Peg's. Judith Wilkins."

"But of course I remember!" he exclaimed with the graciousness of a great actor meeting one of his fans. "Poor darling Peg! Too devastating. I simply couldn't take it in when I heard it. As though anyone could possibly—and there was no one who profited— Oh, dear, you must forgive me! I'm afraid tact isn't my strong suit."

Judy suddenly had the impression that she was trying to hold a dangerous dog on the leash, and her hand tightened warningly on Jon's arm. "This is Jonathan Fullbright. Maxwell Allington, Peg's cousin. We caught your show this afternoon." She was pretty sure that was the right phrase.

Maxwell brushed his hand through his hair with the boyish gesture that he used in each performance to mark the climax of the picture. "How sweet of you!"

"We came here right away." Judy fixed wide eyes on his face. "We've turned ourselves into a committee of two to find out who killed Peg. We thought perhaps you could help us."

Maxwell backed away a couple of steps. "Well, I'm sure—I don't suppose—of course I hadn't seen darling Peg in months—but anyhow—"

"You do better," Jonathan said unkindly, "when someone writes your lines."

6

"Well, really," Maxwell began indignantly. "Why the two of you—"

"You're the next of kin," Fullbright told him. "You can't ignore it, you know."

"But Judy rakes in every penny," Maxwell said rather shrilly. "If what I read in the paper is true, every penny. One wonders why, you know."

Judy was more aware than before that she was holding back a dangerous man. She had been mistaken in thinking he was patient.

"Why," Jon asked her, "why do you think she left it to you?"

"She said, the last time I talked to her, that I was the only person she really trusted," Judy replied, and then stared, owl-eyed, at Maxwell Allington.

"Well, really!" he said again, but somehow he wasn't convincing. "I can tell you this. I hadn't seen Peg in months. Not in months. We weren't at all congenial. She was the least sympathetic, the least understanding —and that cruel, brittle tongue of hers! Anyhow, why are you acting like this, coming to me, one of the most peaceful, least grasping of men—and the paper said it was a burglar. You can hardly believe I am a burglar."

They couldn't, of course, and Judy agreed mentally that he was both peaceful and ungrasping. But something disturbed Maxwell.

"Have you ever," Jon asked, "heard of an actress named Dolores Costanza?"

Maxwell did not move at all. He seemed to have

frozen in the position in which he stood. His face was without expression. Only his eyes moved. And the color seemed to seep out of his lips. "It seems to me I have heard of her," he said, after too long an interval. "Seen her around."

"Around where?" Jon asked.

"Oh, around the station. Coming off sets now and then. I think she did commercials once in a while." He explained to the uninitiated, "Telling people about soap, you know, and shampoos—well, perhaps she was a bit long in the tooth for that; mouthwashes and things to hold in dentures, perhaps."

"You didn't know her yourself?" Jon asked.

After an interval Maxwell said, "We—nodded." Again an interval that was too long, as though he kept forgetting his lines and had to be prompted. "As one does, of course. She was once fairly good, I understand, but years before my time. I wasn't too surprised when I heard of her suicide."

"Suicide?" Jon asked.

Maxwell spread uncertain hands. "Accident, perhaps. She drank, my dears. Not even safe for a bit part. Never knew whether she'd walk on or reel on."

"Accident," Jon repeated thoughtfully. "Or murder? She was afraid she would be murdered. She—told someone." He took advantage of Maxwell being thrown off balance. "Where were you about five o'clock yesterday afternoon?"

Maxwell's mouth opened and closed. Then he said, "You ought to know. You caught my show today. Five afternoons a week. Same time. Same station." Which seemed to be that. Not that Judy found it conceivable that Maxwell had been involved in Dolores Costanza's death.

"I understand from her landlady that she was expecting a windfall," Jon said idly.

Maxwell's glass tipped, spilling Bloody Mary on the table and over onto the rug.

He "tut-tutted," mopped up the mess with a handkerchief discreetly scented with a man's perfume. He did not seem to be in a hurry to finish the job. "A windfall. Well, she could have used it," he said at length when his insensitive guests remained watching him, waiting for him to talk. "Poor thing. But where it would come from—" He dropped the stained handkerchief distastefully in a wastebasket, waved his hands.

"I don't think there's much doubt about that, do you?" Jon said.

Maxwell had rather pale eyes and they were narrowed now to slits, like a cat's in sunlight. "What do you mean?"

"She was a blackmailer," Jon said quietly. "At least she would have been if—she had been given the chance."

II

The restaurant was air-cooled and quiet. There were booths, the service was quiet and unassertive, and the food was superlative.

Jon had thrust Judy into a booth, ordered gin and tonics, and, when they had finished their first drink, ordered refills. Only while they were sipping the second in a leisurely and revived sort of way did he allow her to speak.

Judy, who had fancied herself as an independent sort of girl, was alarmed at what was happening to her. She did not merely accept Jon's leadership; she wallowed in it. For a girl who, at any minute, was going to be left more alone than ever before in her life, this was a perilous attitude to adopt and she knew it. But, having suspended judgment, she thought she might as well do it thoroughly.

Jon suggested the petite marmite, the coq au vin, led her deftly through the menu—this, he explained, was a convenient restaurant, so he dined here a lot when he could not avoid being in New York—and then he smiled at her.

"Feel better?"

"I don't know," she admitted. "Cooler? Yes. More rested? Yes. Otherwise—I don't know. So much has happened today and I don't seem to understand any of it, except that Peg is dead. Horribly dead. She—" Her voice broke, began to rise.

Jon's hand covered hers for a moment. Then he signaled the watchful waiter and ordered a bottle of white wine. There wasn't, she thought, much to read in his rather blunt features. This time yesterday he had been only a voice on the telephone. Now he was apparently taking things over—she did not define to herself what things—and she was sitting back, letting him do it without protest.

The soup was so good that Judy discovered she was ravenous. Over the coq au vin, with tiny browned potatoes and peas, with a crisp salad and hot rolls and iced coffee, she began to revive. Jon did not try to talk much, but when the white wine came in its bucket of ice, he kept her glass filled. He was a pleasantly peaceful man to be with. Except, she remembered, when they had called on Maxwell. Then she had realized how easy it would be for him to get off the leash.

While they waited for coffee, she found that she was able to think about the things that had happened, to talk about them.

"But I don't understand," she said. "Why blackmail?"

"I can't see any other answer. Whatever Dolores Costanza had in that briefcase, it wasn't money or jewelry. She was obviously dead broke. She didn't have a job. She was behind in her rent. But I agree with you about the Collins woman. She wouldn't listen to hard-luck stories and let people stay there for free. So?"

So, he speculated, Dolores Costanza, having come to the end of her rope, had attempted desperate measures. The only possible answer seemed to be blackmail. Her landlady had obviously been afraid when she first saw Judy and Jon that they were on Dolores's pitch. Then, when she showed them her room she had said something about their coming too late, so she must have assumed they, too, were victims. One thing sure. Mrs. Collins had been afraid of Dolores. That unpaid rent meant that the actress had some sort of hold on her.

And that, Jon admitted, could be on practically any charge. It would be easier to list the things the Collins woman couldn't do than those she might easily be capable of. On the other hand, it was possible that the "windfall" she had mentioned was a fact. Someone had promised Dolores money. And someone had found a cheaper way of canceling the debt.

It wasn't, Judy argued, all that obvious. It seemed to her mostly guesswork. "And how," she asked in discouragement, "do we find out whom she was blackmailing when we don't have the briefcase and, presumably, the documents or letters or whatever evidence she had against someone?"

"We could start with Maxwell. He got the shock of his life when Dolores came into the conversation."

"I refuse to consider Maxwell. He's waspish and ungenerous, but he wouldn't kill anyone."

"Too cowardly?"

"No," she said. "He just isn't a violent man."

"Anyone can, in certain circumstances, be a violent man."

She shook her head. "Speak for yourself. I've an idea that you could be a very violent man."

"I," he assured her, "am a man of letters. Withdrawn. Remote. Sedentary. Solitary. Purely the mental type." He studied her doubtfully. "A professional writer who lives alone and likes it."

"I do wish," Judy said rather resentfully, "you'd stop throwing out all that smoke screen. You don't do it like a writer; you do it like a—like a squid hiding itself in its own ink."

"A bachelor," he amplified, "fighting for his freedom."

"Well, you don't have to fight me. And how did we get on this, anyhow? We were talking about blackmail."

"So we were," he said amiably. "And Maxwell. Suppose—"

"I won't suppose." Judy was firm. "I absolutely refuse to believe Maxwell would kill anyone, would ever think of killing anyone, no matter what."

"But—"

"No," she said.

Unexpectedly Jon smiled at her. "All right. We still have a pretty wide field."

"We have?"

"Taking them in order, from the landlady's account, we have, first, her ex-husband."

"But that marriage was broken up years ago," Judy protested.

"And he remarried. Yes, I remember. Just the same, I insist that we consider the husband. And his second wife."

"I think that is silly."

"Men," Jon commented reflectively, "usually enjoy a little more appreciation." As Judy snorted in an unladylike way, he abandoned the subject. "Then we have the man who broke up his own marriage because of her. And his wife."

"I suppose we just advertise for them," Judy said dryly. "Will the man who broke up Dolores Costanza's marriage umteen years ago please step forward and give an account of himself?"

"At least it would be a nice, direct approach," Jon said approvingly. He refilled her wine glass.

"Hey," she protested, "I don't usually have much to drink. In fact, practically nothing."

"Do you good. Then, and for my money the best bet, we have the man who stole money to buy diamond earrings for Dolores, went to prison for theft, and scared hell out of her by being released. A man like that could carry a grudge for a long, long time."

"But Mrs. Collins didn't remember any names."

"My first reaction," he said coolly, "would be the gossip columnists who covered the Broadway beat from ten to thirty years ago. Give us a nice broad range and some juicy reading material." He glanced at the bill, pulled out a startling amount of money, and helped her slide out of the booth. "But my immediate suggestion would be bed."

Judy turned to him in surprise. He was grinning.

"My intentions," he informed her, "are strictly honorable. At least for the time being. I make no predictions for the future. You are an entrancing child, but I am not a marrying man, so we start without any misconceptions. And at the moment you are practically out on your feet."

"Well, what," Judy said indignantly, "can you expect if you ply a girl with liquor on a hot night when she's worn-out and not accustomed to drinking?"

"So," he ignored this comment, "I am going to take you to my apartment. You don't want to go to your own, and I don't blame you for that. Anyhow, I'd rather have an eye on you."

What had been idle banter was suddenly no longer amusing. "You think that—tail—is still following me?"

"Let's say I'm the overly cautious type who doesn't take chances. Not, at least, with a small girl with fluffy hair and what I suspect is a calculatedly misleading appearance of helplessness. Come on. My apartment is just around the corner."

It was, actually, only two blocks away, an old converted building, set, in the confusing way of New York architecture, between a new high-rise apartment building and an old decaying house that rented out furnished rooms.

Jon had the second floor of a walk-up, with a charming and comfortable living room, a small bedroom, bath, and kitchenette. He removed pajamas from the bedroom and said, "You'll find clean towels in the bathroom and the sheets were changed today. I'll clean my teeth first and leave you in peace."

He turned back the bed for her, opened the window, and said, "Sorry about the fire escape at the back. It doesn't add much to the view, but the law requires it. I don't use this place much. In fact, I never come to New York if I can avoid it; only when I am gathering material. If you want anything, give a yell."

"Well, I—"

"Oh." He came back to open a dresser drawer, pull out clean pajamas, and unhook a bathrobe from the bathroom door. He gave her a half smile. "These won't be much of a fit, but they'll do in an emergency." He checked the words on her lips by saying, "Don't hold it against me if I refuse to make an honest woman of you as a result of this. That's fair warning." He gave a villain's laugh.

"Why, you—" she began indignantly.

He grinned at her and closed the door. When she had brushed her teeth and put on Jon's pajamas, which, as he had predicted, did not fit very well, she slid between the cool sheets. Of all the incredible—of all—she heard the springs of the living room couch protest as Jon lay on them. She wondered dimly what Peg would think if she knew she was spending the night in the apartment of a man she had not met twenty-four hours ago.

A pale moon etched in black the fire escape outside the window. Judy lay staring at it, thinking of Peg with her face emptied of expression, of the abortive trip to Danbury and the elusive moving van that might be anywhere, but was certainly somewhere, moving farther and farther west and out of reach. And with every stop the chances of retrieving the briefcase would become more remote.

She thought of Dolores Costanza and her fear. "I am being watched." Somewhere near them on the subway someone had watched, someone who had shoved the woman onto the express tracks. Someone who then found and murdered Peg.

Blackmail. Mrs. Collins had been afraid and so had Maxwell, but Judy still refused to suspect Maxwell. Anyhow, he had an unbreakable alibi. How many more suspects had Jon mentioned? Jon was turning restlessly on his side; she could hear the springs creak again and she smelled smoke as he lighted another cigarette. Jon, who had refused to leave her all day long. Judy found herself smiling in a kind of contentment.

And then the moon disappeared. Perhaps behind a cloud? There were only shadows where the moonlight had been, a deeper shadow at the window.

Judy struggled, trying to get the pillow off her face, to get air into her lungs. Her legs thrashed, one arm struck the end table beside the bed and knocked it over. If it made any sound, Judy could not hear. There was nothing to hear but the noises in her own head, the banging of her heart. There was pain, searing pain, in her chest.

And then, dimly, there was a crash, the pillow was gone and the pressure, and her laboring lungs began to gulp air. There was light that hurt her eyes and a thud. And then Jon was cursing softly to himself, was running back from the window to the living room, dialing a number.

He was calling a doctor, Judy realized dimly, and then the police. None of it mattered. Nothing mattered at all but filling her lungs, breathing in the carbon monoxide and the gas fumes and the smog that pass for air in New York, and rejoicing in them.

The doctor, as it happened, lived in the next building. He beat the police by only a couple of minutes.

When he removed the stethoscope and sat back in his chair, he studied Judy with unconcealed curiosity. "What happened to you?"

Jon, who had caught up the dressing gown he had left for her, shrugged into it. "Is she all right?"

"A few bruises on her face and throat, but she'll be all right. What happened?"

"It's my fault," Jon said bitterly. "I never thought of the fire escape constituting a danger. I should have locked that window and kept the door to the living room open for air."

There was a familiar voice and Judy's heart sank.

"Well," Lieutenant Krill exclaimed as he saw Judy in Jon's bed. At the expression on Jon's face, Judy was aware again that he was not a patient, easygoing young man.

"Jon!" she said warningly, and the anger faded.

He smiled at her. "Okay, youngster. Have it your own way." He was under control now, but he was still angry. Angry with himself. He made that clear. "I knew Miss Wilkins would be in danger. And she didn't want to go back to that apartment where— Anyhow, I brought her here so I could keep an eye on her. Not enough of an eye, apparently. I was sleeping on the living room couch." He glared at the lieutenant, daring him to challenge the remark.

"Sure you were," Krill agreed pleasantly. "Sure. So what happened?"

"Someone got in through the window on the fire escape and tried to smother her with a pillow. What aroused me was the crash when the end table was knocked over. I gave a shout, and when Judy didn't answer, I went running. We tangled in the dark, he tripped me up and got out the window."

Krill arched eyebrows at the doctor, who nodded. "What it looks like. Someone tried to smother the young lady with a pillow. All right now, of course, bar a few bruises and some shock."

Krill went out of the bedroom to issue orders. "Though the chances of finding anyone still hanging around are slight. How long ago was it?"

"I was called twelve minutes ago, and I've been here eight," the doctor said.

"Call it thirteen." Jon said curtly. "I tore off the pillow and the guy got away. He had a stocking tied over his face. Nothing to recognize, dark as it was."

"Yeah." Krill looked from Jon to Judy again. "You are sure someone got in by the window?"

She was bewildered. The soft light hair curled tight by dampness made her look about sixteen. "Well, that's the only way he could have come, except through the living room."

"Yeah."

Her eyes searched his face. "You mean—Jon?"

"How well do you know this guy, Miss Wilkins?"

"You ought to know. You introduced us. And don't be so silly!"

"Where have you two been today? And what makes you think, Fullbright, that Miss Wilkins is in danger?"

"You ought to know where we've been. Your man followed us all day long."

The lieutenant shook his head. "I didn't have anyone following you, Fullbright." He turned to Judy. "Did you see anyone following you?"

"No," she admitted, "no, I didn't."

7

"She's good for eight hours," the doctor said as he put away the hypodermic. "Ought to be all right tomorrow." He picked up his bag, his curiosity unappeased about the quiet girl on the bed, about the angry young man in the fiery red dressing gown, about the amiable man in plain clothes who had introduced himself as Lieutenant Krill of Homicide.

"Will you or will you not leave a man on guard?" Jon demanded.

"Locking the stable," Krill commented.

"You don't know that. Well, if you won't, you won't. I'll spend the night in here with the window locked on the fire escape and a chair propped under the front door. Unfortunately I am a peaceful citizen. No guns. No knives." He looked about as peaceful as a bushmaster.

"Okay," the lieutenant capitulated, and ordered a man to stand guard at the foot of the fire escape. A search of the roof and the neighborhood had not turned up any lurking stranger, but then he had not expected that it would. This wasn't the kind of case Krill liked. He wasn't used to dealing with amateurs, and there wasn't much hope of a squeal from someone. In Jon's living room he sat down rather tiredly and accepted a cigarette. After a hesitation he accepted coffee.

"What's all this about, Fullbright? So far as I can learn from *New Trends,* you never heard of the Morrison girl until yesterday."

Jon nodded, tipped ashes into a big tray.

"And you never saw the roommate, this Wilkins girl, until this morning."

Jon nodded again.

"So," Krill said, "I don't get it. I checked you out. Way up there in your profession. You earn more annually than the Morrison girl inherited. You've got a private income besides from some aunt, nearly another forty thousand a year. So—why?"

Jon drank coffee, raised polite eyebrows.

"Why, I mean," Krill said patiently, "are you leading with your chin to look after this kid? Getting mixed up in murder. Mixed up maybe with a murderess."

He hadn't, Jon said, keeping his voice level, involved himself in murder by malice aforethought. He had, almost literally, stumbled into it. Maybe that was why, when he saw what had been done to Miss Morrison, the savage way her head had been beaten in, a helpless girl, he had taken a hand. Let's say, at least, he had decided to keep an eye on Judy. He had thought she was in danger, which, he pointed out, seemed to be verified by the attempt on her tonight.

Jon shook his head as Krill began to speak. "And I didn't," he said, "attempt to smother Judy Wilkins in my own apartment and my own bed. If I had had such intention, I'd have done it far, far away, and then failed to call a doctor and the policeman. Though I am not, Lieutenant, a violent man."

Like Judy, Krill questioned this. The violence was there in that powerful, compact body, controlled perhaps, but there. It was in the face that was, somehow, stripped for action.

"Anyhow," Jon demanded, "why?"

"That's what I want to know. The only motive I can see here is profit. The Wilkins girl is the only one who stands to gain, and she gains plenty. She hadn't a penny of her own until she sold her cottage yesterday, and she didn't get enough out of that to keep her more than a few months."

"No," Jon told him. "No, Judy didn't kill her room-mate."

Krill drank his coffee, refused, regretfully, a high-ball, watched enviously while Jon mixed one for him-self, the tinkle of ice against the long glass an irritation in the hot, sultry night.

"All right," Krill said, "give me someone else."

Jon lighted another cigarette, opened the bedroom door and looked in. Judy was breathing evenly, her hair and face pale in the moonlight that was shining in once more.

Krill watched him. "You really are anxious about her." He sounded surprised.

"She's in danger. If you don't know it now, what would convince you?"

"Look here." Krill tried to be reasonable. "We have a pretty clear-cut situation. A wealthy girl leaves everything she has to her penniless roommate. Then she is conked on the head in an apartment building where tenants don't open their doors to people they don't know, especially when they aren't announced. And the roommate hasn't an alibi that will stand up. She had plenty of time to kill Morrison and get up to Danbury before we found her. The trooper there tried to reach her by telephone three times before he finally ran her down. So?" He looked hopefully at Jon, who shook his head.

"What about this deal tonight?" Jon demanded. "Do you think Judy staged that?"

"Who's to say that she didn't?"

"Tripping me up, getting out of the window, and all the time lying in bed. Quite a trick. Houdini couldn't have brought that off."

"Okay, like I said, give me someone else."

Jon drank and set down his glass. He gave the lieu-tenant cousin Maxwell, who had turned out to be Max-well Allington, actor in a daily television program. He admitted that he wasn't giving him much. Max-well had an alibi for the time of the murder; in fact, he was appearing in a television play at the time.

70

"It seems to me," the lieutenant said plaintively, "that you or Miss Wilkins might have told me who this Maxwell is. Let us do our own job. But if the guy has an alibi, let's throw him back."

"You mean that you won't check on him?" Jon asked in surprise.

"Oh, sure we'll check." Krill was equally surprised. "But he didn't inherit. He has an alibi. I can't see motive or opportunity. I can't see a damned thing but a mighty faded red herring."

Jon finished the highball, pushed away his glass. He gave the lieutenant Dolores Costanza and the briefcase. Marshaling his facts neatly, he provided a blow-by-blow account of Judy's encounter with the actress on the subway, the exchange of briefcases, and the day he and Judy had just spent in an attempt to retrieve it.

There was a definite connection between the two deaths, the two murders, Jon insisted. Costanza's room at the "family hotel" had been torn apart in the same way as the Morrison apartment, drawers overturned, bedding stripped back. Same technique.

As an afterthought, Jon gave Krill Mrs. Collins, but not hopefully. No seventy-year-old woman had tripped him up and scrambled down the fire escape.

While Krill brooded, Jon got up to mix himself another highball. This time, after only a token resistance, the lieutenant joined him.

"Blackmail. It explains just about everything," Jon said. "Why the woman was killed but the briefcase was missing. Why Peg Morrison was the only person whose apartment was burgled. Her name and address, even her apartment number, were pasted in her own briefcase, which had been in the possession of Dolores Costanza at the time of her death. Why, after Judy's name got in the news, someone tried to get the briefcase from her by a faked telephone call. Why someone followed us all day. Why someone tried to kill her tonight."

Krill pulled a cigarette out of a battered pack,

crumpled the package, looked around for a wastebasket and finally dropped it in the big ashtray. "You think blackmail," he said at last. So they had come full circle.

"What else? Mrs. Collins was scared of us in the beginning, and that gave me the first inkling. She thought we were on the same pitch. She let Costanza stay there rent-free the last couple of months, and yet I think she was telling the truth or part of the truth about that windfall Costanza was so confidently expecting." Jon thought for a moment. "And it explains dear Maxwell being so upset. He didn't want any part of Costanza. He didn't want to talk about her. He had some acutely unpleasant association with her. A blind man could have seen that."

Krill finished his drink, set down his glass, and got up. "Suppose," he suggested mildly, perhaps mellowed by the Scotch, "you leave the case to the police. We quite often know our jobs, Mr. Fullbright."

"Without us you wouldn't even have a case," Jon said, "at least one that links Costanza with Miss Morrison."

"We still haven't, except, if I may express myself in a literary manner, in the realm of fantasy."

"Do you believe a single word I've been saying?" Jon demanded.

"Damned," Krill admitted, "if I know."

II

It hurt to swallow. Judy lifted a hand that was unexpectedly heavy to her throat, swallowed again. Her chest felt raw, as though she had been running uphill on a cold day with her mouth open. But it wasn't cold. Actually, she discovered, she was too warm. Her unexpectedly heavy hand fumbled with a sheet, pushed it aside.

She was aware then that something was different

and opened her eyes, though her lids resisted, were un-
willing to get a look at the new day. It was the pajama
sleeve she noticed first, with unfamiliar green and
white stripes. She studied the sleeve vaguely, then with
more alertness. She saw the odd pattern outside the
window, made by shadows of a fire escape.

And then, in a kind of rush, it all came back to her,
the shadow at the window blotting out the moonlight,
the pillow blotting out air, the agony of trying to
breathe. There had been other things, other faces,
other voices. There had, she remembered clearly, been
Lieutenant Krill. There had been a most revealing
look in his face when he saw Judy in Jon's bed, wear-
ing Jon's pajamas.

To her surprise, a momentary indignation was fol-
lowed by a feeling of: Well, why not? That's what I
would think, too. Poor Jon. Remembering his reiterat-
ed and anxious declaration of independence, she
grinned maliciously to herself. Poor Jon!

She was drifting back to sleep when it occurred to
her to look at her watch. It was after nine. She got up,
moving carefully because her legs did not seem at first
to be under her orders. Then they remembered what
they were supposed to do and carried her to the bath-
room. Because she felt oddly dizzy, she did not dare
risk the shower and took a tub bath. When she had
dressed, she stood on tiptoe to look in the bathroom
mirror—there was none in Jon's bedroom—and tried
to make some running repairs on her face.

She was about to tap cautiously on the door to the
living room when there was a knock from the other
side.

"Jon?" she called. "I was just going to wake you."

"I," he replied in a tone of moral superiority that
was infuriating, "have been up for hours. Do you want
some coffee?"

She opened the door. Except for shaving, Jon
looked neat and prepared for the day. His pajamas had
been folded at the foot of the couch.

"There's coffee in the kitchen," he told her. "I was just going to get breakfast. Eggs and bacon. I hope you like them, because that's all there is."

"I'll fix them," she offered. "Boiled, fried or scrambled?"

While bacon sputtered in the pan, she heard the sound of the electric shaver in the bathroom, a normal domestic sound in any normal household, except, of course, that this one wasn't. She was probably giving too much importance to the whole situation because Jon, when he appeared, freshly shaven and wearing a clean white shirt, was matter-of-fact. Rather determinedly matter-of-fact, she realized after a few minutes, which, for some reason, she found reassuring.

"Did they find him?" she asked at last.

He shook his head and reached for salt, sprinkling the eggs lavishly.

"You'll get hardening of the arteries or something," she said, "if you use that much salt."

"They are my arteries."

"Well, you can keep them, hard or soft. They are nothing to me. What did the police find?"

"Nobody. No clues."

"What does Lieutenant Krill think?"

"To start with, I rather imagine he thought I was trying to strangle you myself." He looked at her thoughtfully. "I can see his point, of course. Then you became his favorite suspect. He really hated to give you up, what with your lovely motive and all, but I gave him alternatives."

Judy put down the piece of toast she had just begun to butter. "You gave him what?"

"I gave him Maxwell."

"But, Jon!"

"And Dolores Costanza. And the briefcase. And Mrs. Collins. The works."

She pushed aside her plate, put her elbows on the table, her chin held cupped in one hand. "What are you doing, Jon? What are you doing?"

"For one thing I'm trying to save my own skin. For

another, but strictly in second place, I'm trying to save yours. I thought the lieutenant needed more scope for his investigations and his suspicions. And I didn't like your little night caller. I didn't like him at all. Not neighborly."

Her eyes widened. "Neither did I." Her hand groped over her throat. "Well? What is Krill going to do about it?"

"So far as I know," Jon admitted, "the lieutenant didn't believe anything I said and he isn't going to do anything about it." And then he was, almost instantly, proved to be mistaken.

The telephone rang and Judy started, spilling her coffee. "Sorry, I guess I'm still sort of nervous."

He lifted the telephone and said, "Fullbright . . . Yes . . . She seems to be all right . . . Oh? . . . Oh! Well, I will be damned!"

He came back to his seat, poured more coffee, buttered more toast, reached for marmalade.

Judy waited until she was afraid of bursting. "All right! Give. I can't bear it any longer."

He laughed at her. "Brace yourself, my child. That was Krill. Apparently he thought it was worth doing some checking, after all." Again he waited while he drank coffee in a leisurely way.

Judy picked up the coffeepot. "If," she threatened, maddened by his calmness, "you don't tell me—"

"Oh, all right. I'll talk. I'll go quietly. Well, it seems friend Maxwell was lying his head off to us last night. That program we saw is filmed. It's so successful that it is repeated periodically, so—"

"So it wasn't necessarily being filmed at five o'clock."

"No, the regular routine is to rehearse mornings and they have the whole thing wrapped up, as a rule, before two in the afternoons."

"So Maxwell doesn't have an alibi for the time when Dolores was pushed off the subway platform or when Peg was killed or—"

"Or when someone tried to smother you last night," Jon agreed. "Maxwell told Krill he was seeing a friend off at La Guardia for Egypt at five-thirty. So far they haven't reached the friend. And, while he couldn't be sorrier about poor darling Dolores, she was nothing to him. The merest speaking acquaintance."

III

When Judy, carefully swathed in a big apron to protect her dress, had done the dishes and made the bed, she said, "You know, I'll have to go back to the apartment. All my clothes except for this dress are there. I'll have to go." She shivered.

He looked at the face that was suddenly colorless. "I'll go along," he said casually, "to carry the suitcases. You have until," he looked at his watch, "twelve-thirty to do your packing. Nearly two hours. Time enough?"

"Why two hours?"

"We have a lunch date. I made it while you were taking your bath."

"We have?"

"The reporter who identified Dolores Costanza at the morgue. It occurred to me that he might have some information we could use, and we have something to bargain with."

"The story of the briefcase?"

He nodded. "My idea is to dangle the bait in front of him. An exclusive story if he'll hold his fire until we give him a release."

"If you think so," she said obediently, and he looked pleased with her, as though a promising pupil had made a good mark. Judy found words about smugness, conceit, and unendurable male superiority crowding to her lips and wisely repressed them.

Jake, the elevator man, took them up. The police had been back again yesterday afternoon, he said. Naturally, the building management was co-operating, but they would be just as pleased when the police abandoned its interest in the Morrison apartment.

Their tenants did not like it. Their tenants were used to the best, and expected privacy, and were willing to pay for it. They didn't like murder.

"Neither," Jon pointed out, "did Miss Morrison," and Jake fell silent.

This morning Judy was careful not to look at the stain on the cream-colored carpet. She went to her own room, packed two suitcases, pulled back the covers on the studio couch and straightened the room. Then she braced herself and went in to restore order to Peg's room and hang neatly the dresses that Peg would not be needing again.

The shrilling of the telephone brought her back to the living room. Yes, this was Miss Wilkins. Why, no, never! Oh, once in a while some kids on a rampage would break windows in the vicinity, but nothing worse had ever happened. Well, she was awfully sorry and hoped it wouldn't happen again. The State Police had asked a lot of questions about her? They had called the New York police? How odd. Well, thank you for telling me and I'm sorry your living in the house has got off to a bad start.

Judy turned to Jon. "Someone broke into my cottage about four this morning and ransacked it. The new owners were so tired from moving that they didn't awaken until the housebreaker was actually in their bedroom, but he got away."

"That's one little man who had a busy day," Jon commented. "Let's hope that this morning he is catching up on sleep and that he'll let us alone for a change."

"At least Lieutenant Krill will know that neither you nor I was near Danbury during the night."

"There's always a bright side," Jon said cheerfully.

The morning was so sultry that breathing was difficult. The air pressed down, muggy, lifeless, heavy. Judy tucked a plastic raincoat into its neat envelope under her arm and went out of the apartment, almost without a backward look, while Jon followed her, carrying the suitcases.

"You're leaving us, Miss Wilkins?" Jake asked when

he saw the suitcases. "I understood—that is, Miss Morrison owned this apartment, you know. I guess it's yours now from what I hear."

"I don't know, Jake. In any case, I haven't any plans."

Jon suggested leaving the suitcases in a dime locker at Grand Central when Judy balked at the idea of using the ones at Times Square. She didn't want to see the place again as long as she could avoid it.

"I reserved a table at Sardi's. I thought we might as well kill two birds with one stone. Someone at Sardi's might remember Costanza, even though it's been a long time. We might pick up something. After all, actors have been flocking there for years."

He had reserved a table for three on the second floor. When he had identified himself, he asked about the actress. The knowledgeable Mr. Sardi shook his head. "I read about the death, but I don't remember the woman. Oh, her name rang a faint bell, but that's all. If she came here, I can't remember seeing her. Certainly not one of our regulars, and there's been no gossip since her death." He smiled. "If there is any, you can always hear it here."

"Well, it was worth trying." Jon did not seem to be discouraged. "Just a shot in the dark, and you can't expect to be on target." He followed Judy upstairs, where a waiter nodded, went ahead to whip a RE-SERVED sign off a table and pull out chairs. A bus boy filled glasses, a waiter brought large menus, and a man said, "Are you Fullbright?"

Jon stood up. "Milton?"

"That's right. John Milton. Optimistic mother. However—" He was tall and rangy, with an amused voice and hair that was unexpectedly gray above a youngish face. He wore a shabby seersucker suit and a flamboyant necktie of broad yellow and blue stripes.

He looked inquiringly at Fullbright and approvingly at Judy. He seemed to be co-operative but wary. He gave a quick, appraising look at the tables around him, nodded to a man at one of them, blew a kiss to a woman at another, stared in surprise at a third.

"My, my," he said, "I ought to do this more often. I didn't know she was back in circulation." He appeared to be a man of wide acquaintance.

"What are you drinking?" Fullbright asked, and the reporter brightened.

"Tom Collins."

After a glance at Judy, Jon told the hovering waiter, "Make it three."

"At this rate," Judy said with foreboding, "I'll become an alcoholic."

"There are worse fates." Milton looked at his hand, which had a slight tremor. "I guess."

"Is that what happened to Dolores Costanza?" Jon asked, and the reporter's face cleared.

"So that's the reason for my fatal attraction, for feeding me and plying me with liquor. I was naturally wondering." He reached absently for a piece of Melba toast. "What's the deal?"

"You tell us what you know about Costanza. We give you an exclusive story, if you wait until we release you."

Milton looked him over. "You're Jonathan Fullbright, *Such Men Are Dangerous* Fullbright? That one?"

"That one."

"A damned good job. Well—"

"Under your hat until you get the word?"

"I don't wear a hat, but—"

Judy nodded to Jon. "You can rely on him," she said confidently.

Milton's eyes screwed nearly shut when he smiled. "A psychologist yet!"

"I can't help being observant."

They sipped Tom Collinses and began to cool off. Judy, wide-eyed, looked at actors who, unlike those at the family hotel, were not "resting," whose faces were so familiar that she found herself on the brink of nodding to several of them.

"They're just like anyone, aren't they?" she commented. "Only—more so."

Milton, who had been watching her in some amusement, grinned appreciatively. "I see what you mean. Now what's all this about Dolores Costanza?"

"The prologue is yours, Judy," Jon told her. "Then we'll leave the flashback to Milton."

"What about the body of the play and the epilogue?" the reporter asked.

"God knows," Jon said. "We don't. We write it as we go. How did you happen to identify the woman?"

"Just routine, and it was the hell of a shock."

In the first place she was just any anonymous body that had been brought into the morgue. Someone who had fallen or jumped under an express train during the rush hours. He had taken a look on the off chance. Only one chance in a thousand, but about that often it paid off. This time it had.

Her face hadn't been much—changed. He was speaking now for Judy's benefit. Not much damaged. There had been something familiar about her, and then it had come back to him. Dolores Costanza, of course. The hell of a shock, he repeated. Because he had seen her not more than a week before. If it hadn't been for that, he would never have associated her with the fallen star of fifteen years earlier.

"You ran into her just a week ago?"

"No, she came to the paper. Got passed along to me. She wanted to know what we'd be willing to pay for a story that would blow things sky-high."

"What things?"

"That's the trouble. I wasn't in a position to make a blind offer, not knowing what was up. She wouldn't tell me. And there's always a risk of libel. Papers have to be more careful these days. Sometimes they catch us but good. A clever lawyer can draw blood where it hurts. So she was coming back to see the city editor."

"When was that?"

"Yesterday," the reporter said gloomily.

8

"I'm one hell of a reporter," Milton said in disgust. "You think the gal was murdered. Blackmail?"

Jon nodded. "What else? Apparently if she lost one market she could open up another by selling to the press."

"I had it right in my hand, her visit to the office, her threat that she could blow things sky-high, her wanting a nice fat sum for it, and then her sudden death just before she was due to show up at the office and tell all. Well, if you feel I can still recognize a story when I see it, let's see what you've got."

At Jon's nod, Judy picked up the story from the subway encounter and the exchange of briefcases to last night's attempt to smother her, while Milton listened, forgetting to eat.

"That's quite a tale," he said at last. As though he could not improve on the phrase he repeated, "Quite a tale." He shook his head as though trying to clear it. "And what do I contribute?"

"You identified her. What do you know about her? We don't know where to start unearthing the people whom she might be blackmailing."

"Just what are you really trying to accomplish?"

"I want," Jon said, "to find out who has killed two women and attempted to kill a third. I want to get him before he gets Judy."

"Because," Judy explained, "there's just no place to hide when I don't know what to hide from, and there doesn't seem to be any other way—"

"Yeah. Well, I'm with you as far as I can go, but I

hate to have to tell you I don't see what I can contribute. I'm the last man who could point the finger and say triumphantly, 'That's the one!' To me Dolores was simply a ghost from the past. I have no idea what people she knew, what she was doing, what she had on whom. And that is the simple and discouraging fact."

"But you have old files," Jon said.

"Oh, sure. That's where I dug up the picture of her. And we always have some stuff on hand for an obit on anyone who gets in the news. I found stuff about her early life, mostly baloney, of course, prepared by a public relations man, but at least we knew her real name was Doris Curtis and she was born in Gary, Indiana, in nineteen-ten. I vaguely remember seeing her in a movie years ago, sultry type. And there were rumors, of course. But nothing that seemed of any importance, nothing that could give you a lead now. She was only a flash in the pan and she faded out quicker than most."

"She didn't stab anyone in the back?"

"Probably. It's a dog-eat-dog profession. That would appear to be how she got ahead. I don't think you can get away from the fact that she was not a nice woman. Not, of course, that nice women don't get themselves killed. But Dolores—I don't know—going over the stuff we had, she struck me somehow as pathetic. She was one of those idiots who get to believe in their own publicity, for whom a carefully fabricated public image becomes reality."

"According to her landlady she had been married and broke up another marriage. Know anything about that?"

"We'll go back to the office and take a look. I didn't do too thorough a job because she wasn't news any more."

"Ever hear of some guy who stole money to buy her diamond earrings and went to prison for it?"

Milton shook his head. "But, you know, I always

get a kind of satisfaction out of finding out that some other jerk has been a bigger fool than I am."

When both Judy and the reporter had refused dessert, Jon said, "All right with you if we take you up on that now?"

"Oh, sure, sure. Come along."

As he had already told them, there was little in the old files about Dolores Costanza. A few photographs, a few reviews of the movies in which she had appeared, a story, brief and played down discreetly in the form of an interview, in which she announced that after her divorce from Elmer Burbank she would marry Gordon Hendricks, the broker. A careful search failed to indicate that Dolores had remarried, but there was a story in the theatrical section of the Sunday paper saying that Ellen Wills, the child actress, was suing Gordon Hendricks for divorce and that she had named Dolores Costanza as corespondent.

"Hell, I remember now," Milton said. "Ellen Wills was the wistful Margaret O'Brien type of child actress. Then as she began to grow up, she couldn't do those parts any more and she began playing ingénue roles, sentimental comedies of calf love, the old Andy Hardy sort of thing."

"Oh," Judy said, "a big swing under the apple trees, an adolescent boy who falls over his own feet, and a girl in fluffy dresses and peals of girlish laughter."

He nodded. "That sort of thing. Anyhow, there had been no previous publicity about Ellen's marriage because it would have spoiled the school-girl image, and her husband was thirty years older than she was. Well, when she announced her divorce, she couldn't keep that innocent young girl buildup. Anyhow, the public loses faith in the glamour girl who can't hold her own husband. Hendricks made a big settlement on her, so our little Ellen is probably doing all right. If she's still alive. Never heard of her since. But Hendricks—and it's just possible you are hitting the jackpot on the first hand around, beginner's luck—Hendricks is up for approval as ambassador somewhere."

"I don't see," Judy admitted, "why a story everyone knew ten or fifteen years ago should do the man any harm now. I don't see how it could blow things sky-high or interfere with his being approved."

"Neither do I," Jon agreed. "What about Dolores's ex-husband, Elmer Burbank?"

"Search me," Milton said. "I never saw the guy. Dolores kept him strictly in the background. He may be dead or in Alaska or standing right behind us now, for all I know."

Judy caught herself glancing uneasily over her shoulder and laughed at herself.

"So what do we do now?" she asked when she and Jon had left Milton at the newspaper office.

"We find a telephone directory and see whether we can run down any interesting people."

While Judy looked at shelves of paperback books in the air-cooled drugstore, Jon wrestled at the back of the store with the huge telephone directories of the five boroughs and kept dodging back and forth to a telephone booth.

When he came toward her at last, she reflected again that his was a difficult face to read. Searching it now, she had no indication whether he had discovered anything or not.

"Well?" she asked eagerly.

"There is no Elmer Burbank in New York. Gordon Hendricks, I learn, has an unlisted number. His former brokerage firm knows him no longer, as he retired several months ago, and I quote without comment, to devote all his energies to the public service. But there is a Mrs. Ellen Hendricks who lives in a nice high-priced apartment hotel on Central Park South. I suggest we extend the range of our acquaintance and meet the lady."

"It wasn't a woman I talked to on the telephone or who ran away from you at the drugstore or who tripped you up last night."

"True, O Queen. But a woman whose husband ditched her for another glamour-puss, causing her to lose her popularity with the public, is apt to have a long, long memory."

"Well, if you think so," she agreed. Her expression changed. "But if you dare—just once more—look as though you were going to pat me on the head approvingly like a well-trained dog getting a reward, I'll—I'll hit you."

Jon grinned at her. "You needn't worry. I don't approve of you in the least." He began to laugh. "You look like a soft fluffy kitten and then you arch your back and spit like a full-grown cat. Pull back those claws, baby."

Judy was still sputtering when he put her in a taxicab and gave an address on Central Park South.

II

"There's one thing sure," Judy said when the doorman opened the taxi with a flourish and had given the revolving door a spin as though they would be unable to accomplish this feat by themselves, "Mrs. Hendricks seems to have the money to pay blackmail. What makes you think she'll see us?"

"Curiosity," Jon said briefly. "It never fails." He added mockingly, "With a woman, that is."

Judy ignored him.

At the desk he gave his name and murmured something vague about *The New York Sentinel*. When the man had spoken briefly over the switchboard telephone, he nodded to Jon. "Eleven Twelve. To your right as you leave the elevator. At the end of the corridor."

On the eleventh floor they turned right, turned right again. At the end of the corridor a uniformed maid waited at an open door.

"Mr. Fullbright?" She glanced curiously at Judy.

"And Miss Wilkins," he said.

"Mrs. Hendricks will see you in just a minute. This way, please." She led them to a small sitting room with a neat desk and a few chairs. The walls were almost papered with autographed photographs and a number of enlarged pictures of a wistful child whom Judy remembered seeing in a tear-jerker on the Late Late Show.

She wandered around the room looking at the photographs. Those from actors were gushingly inscribed, but most of them were of Ellen Hendricks herself, either as the small charmer or as the young girl of fifteen years ago.

Jon looked over the room, looked out of the window and down on Central Park, on Fifth Avenue to the right and Central Park West to the left. Very nice, he thought. Very, very nice. Mrs. Hendricks' alimony must be quite a bundle. Quite a weight for a man to carry.

The building was so well insulated that it was only when a door opened that the sound of women's voices raised in chatter and laughter could be heard. Then it was shut again.

"Mr. Fullbright?" a girl asked.

She was not a girl at all. She was, perhaps, thirty-five. But her hair styling was a girl's, her voice and mannerisms were a girl's, her mini skirt was a girl's, and not suited to legs that were heavy in proportion to her body.

She looked at Judy and back at Jon, a question in her face. "No photographer?"

Jon grinned. "No photographer," he said cheerfully. "We know you must dislike very much having old scandals raked up, old stories revived. We are going to handle all this as tactfully as possible, but it seems only fair to let you tell us your side of the story."

There was a shade of disappointment that vanished at once. She held out her hand in a pretty, appealing, girlish way. "How sweet! How understanding! I suppose," and her expression wasn't girlish at all, "you've come about the suicide of poor old Dolores. But I'm afraid there is nothing I can tell you. I hadn't heard of her existence in years, except now and then I saw her on television doing some cheesy commercial." She caught the shrillness in her voice, and it became sweet again.

"But you did name her when you divorced Mr. Hendricks."

"Well, what else could I do? She made an out-and-out fool of him. He even went to opening nights with her instead of taking me. Everyone was talking about it. He just lost his head. But when it came right down to it," and her eyes narrowed, her tongue licked out over her lips, "he made a fool of her, too. He never married her, you know, though she divorced Elmer Burbank to get him. I could have told her that Gordon could be led on a leash but he couldn't be pushed around. He'd just balk. He could be stubborn as a mule." She laughed, and her laughter was cruel.

"What a pity," Judy broke in with her wide-eyed look, "after such a misunderstanding, you and Mr. Hendricks couldn't come together again."

"Well, I don't know." Ellen seemed rather amused. "He was a good thirty years older than I am, which is one reason why we never mentioned the marriage while I was acting. People don't understand these—attractions." She put a handkerchief to dry eyes. "Anyhow, I got a lump-sum settlement that would make the eyes of some women bug out, I can tell you. And now I do just what I want to, play bridge and go shopping. I never really liked acting, all that memorizing, and the lights hurt my eyes. And no more marriage for me, thank you! You get a bunch of kids and lose your youth."

"Then you haven't seen your ex-husband recently?" Jon asked.

"Heavens, not in years to talk to. Of course now and then I've run into him at a restaurant or in a theater lobby between acts, and we nod. I hear he's trying to get made ambassador somewhere. Give me New York any time, but if that's what he wants, more power to him."

"To get back to Dolores Costanza," Jon said.

"Look! The old—witch is dead. Let's forget her."

"I was wondering; you spoke as though you had known her first husband, Elmer Burbank."

"Well, it's his wife, really, his second wife. You people want a drink?"

Judy shook her head. Ellen lighted one cigarette from another, rings flashing in the sunlight as she did so.

"His second wife?" Jon prompted.

He never gives up, Judy thought. He doesn't act important or anything, but he never gives up.

"It was funny in a way. I was playing in a bridge tournament, and I met this woman, a Mrs. Elmer Burbank. We clicked right off, though she's a lot older than I am, but we both adore bridge and we got to talking. I said something about knowing an Elmer Burbank once, married to an old has-been actress, Dolores Costanza, and she was sort of stiff and said that was her husband."

Judy, looking at Jon, thought his very ears seemed to vibrate like radio antennae.

"Well, I mean I made clear right off that Dolores had been no friend of mine, that she had broken up my happy marriage, and that I remembered Elmer as being sort of cute. Big, kind of ruddy-faced guy, an athlete at college, all man. And she said he was still like that. He's an account executive with Melcher and O'Brien. Hazel Burbank and I lunch at the Colony now and then, but she stays mostly at their house in Westchester. They have a couple of kids in private schools and all like that. You know—conservative. But it was kind of funny running into her that way. I'll bet," and this time the viciousness cut through that linkéd sweetness long drawn out, "Elmer Burbank is one person who didn't shed any tears when Dolores got it. She just flaunted Gordon right before his eyes."

"So far as we can make out," Judy said, "no one shed any tears for Dolores Costanza."

"Oh, that reminds me," Jon said, getting to his feet, glancing at Judy, "there was some story, some rumor, that a man stole money to buy diamonds for Dolores and that he went to prison for it. Do you happen to know who that could be?"

"The earrings!" Ellen began to laugh. "You know that's kind of funny, too. Those earrings were really what broke us up. Gordon and me, I mean. There was a big first night, I don't remember what it was now, and Gordon took Dolores. I had to dig out my public relations man and read him the riot act. He had another date and I made him break it and take me on account of a star like me couldn't go without an escort. That would be the absolute end. All my best friends laughing their heads off. Well, I mean to say. Anyhow, there was Dolores wearing those earrings. Diamonds. Practically down to her shoulders. I was mad enough to spit. I told Gordon what I thought. Here I was, young and just a kid and real cute. Everyone thought so. And he was an old guy who might act reasonable. And he was spending money on that—on that—and he swore up and down he had never given her any diamonds."

"Then you don't know who gave them to her."

"Oh, yes, I do. And if I don't exactly know I can guess. You wait a minute and I'll show you. I'll just tell the girls to go on without me for the next rubber."

"Well," Judy began when Ellen had gone out. Jon shook his head violently at her. A door opened and again they heard women's voices, raised in laughter and chatter. The door closed. Another door along the hall opened—there must, Jon estimated, be at least eight rooms in the apartment—drawers opened and were slammed impatiently shut and then Ellen returned.

"I knew I had it somewhere." She opened a big scrapbook and Jon's heart sank as he saw that it apparently covered the career of that lovely child actress, Ellen Wills, but she turned pages rapidly, flipped the book over to the back. "I got this stuff just in case I'd need it for the divorce," she said, "but Gordon didn't contest. And anyhow—here! I knew it."

She pushed the open album toward Jon, who followed her pointing finger. There were several pictures of Dolores Costanza. In one of them she appeared triumphant in evening dress, the diamond earrings dangling, as Ellen had said, almost to her bare shoulders. She was autographing albums for fans. Behind her stood a distinguished-looking man in his fifties, in evening dress, looking on in amusement.

"That's Dolores with Gordon. And those are the diamonds. Now," Ellen took back the album and turned pages feverishly, "see?"

It was a candid camera shot of Dolores turning to smile from the open window of a car. In this picture there were no earrings. She wore street dress. Jon looked a question at Ellen. "I don't see—"

"The driver," she pointed out. "The man at the wheel. I was trying to get stuff on Dolores at the time on account of Gordon. I thought it would help if he knew she was two-timing him."

"But he knew," Judy asked in surprise, "didn't he, that she was married?"

"Oh, him?" Ellen shrugged. "But this was different. Elmer was a kid she married when he didn't have anything and she didn't know her own possibilities. But this was different. I think she really fell for this guy."

"Who is he?"

"I was having him followed," Ellen said, "is how I got this picture. The man's name is Hugh Allison. He was a bank clerk and a beautiful guy, though the picture of him is too dim for you to see him clearly. You wouldn't think a guy who looked like that would need to buy diamonds. I mean like Cary Grant or something. Anyhow, three months later he was arrested for rigging the books at his bank or something like that. He had stolen the money to buy diamonds for Dolores. He went up for three years."

"You," Jon told her gravely, "have been invaluable, Mrs. Hendricks. I can't tell you how grateful we are. You don't happen to know what happened to this Allison after he served his sentence, do you?"

She shook her head. "I was divorced by then, so it didn't matter to me any more. Anyhow, Dolores," and her tongue licked over her lips, "was but definitely on the skids. No, it didn't matter any more."

"I suppose not," Jon agreed. "Thank you very much, Mrs. Hendricks."

"That's all right. It's been kind of queer, digging this up again. With Gordon going in for a diplomatic post he wouldn't like this mess raked over in the press. He wouldn't like it at all. And I've nothing against Gordon any more. After all, I'm sitting pretty. Whatever you say for Gordon, he was generous."

"Do you have any idea how I could reach him? His telephone is unlisted."

"I haven't any idea where he lives now, but he always spent a lot of time at the Royal Flush Club. Crazy about poker. Say, why are we raking all this up anyhow?"

"Because," Jon said, "we believe Dolores Costanza was murdered."

She stared at him blankly, and Jon took half a step forward. If he expected Ellen Wills Hendricks to faint under the shock, he was mistaken. "Well!" After a moment she repeated, "Well! You know it couldn't have happened to a nicer person. Oh, by the way, if you should need any pictures of me, I have some. Real cute. Glossies."

9

The Royal Flush Club occupied the fifth floor of a Park Avenue apartment building, and it was obviously designed for gambling on a lavish scale. After a quick look at the plush interior and the well-equipped bar, Jon reflected that Gordon Hendricks had to be well-heeled to play here. In equipment it resembled a small but complete Monte Carlo.

At this hour the big reception room with its inviting couches, deep soft chairs and subdued lighting was deserted. The man who admitted them was quiet in appearance, with cold observant eyes and unexpectedly powerful shoulders. On occasion he probably doubled as a bouncer in a gentlemanly sort of way.

"Mr. Hendricks? I couldn't say. Who is asking for him?"

"Fullbright. *The New York Sentinel.*"

The cold eyes studied Fullbright more intently. "Our members don't see reporters here. Sorry." He turned toward the door.

Fullbright pulled out a notebook and scrawled: "I'd like a word with you about Dolores Costanza. This is purely personal."

The man hesitated and then shrugged. "I'll see whether Mr. Hendricks is here."

He came back almost at once, followed by a man in his late sixties, distinguished, every inch an ambassador in appearance, so much so that it was difficult to believe in him at all, strictly type casting.

"Fullbright?"

"I am Fullbright. Miss Wilkins, Mr. Hendricks."

"How do you do? How about a drink?"

Judy shook her head emphatically and Fullbright declined for them both.

"Iced coffee?" Hendricks gave an order to the waiting—and watchful—man. When he had gone, he waved them to chairs. "How'd you run me down here?" he asked.

"We've just come from your ex-wife. She suggested that we might find you here."

Hendricks smoothed out Jon's note. "Dolores Costanza. What's all this about?"

"We wondered whether you had been in communication with her recently, sir."

Hendricks paused, his lighter hovering over his cigarette. Then it made contact, he inhaled, and put the lighter away. "Miss Costanza," he said, his tone mellifluous, his eyes watchful, "is a voice from the past. It is many years since I have seen her."

"You know, of course, of her tragic death."

"I saw the story in the paper. Sad, very sad. But, after so long a time, of course, one's memories fade, one's impressions grow dim."

"But at one time," Fullbright smiled, "the impression she made must have been fairly vivid."

"I suppose you have a valid reason for bringing up this extremely distasteful matter," Hendricks said.

"It seems valid to us," Jon told him. "There is every reason to believe Dolores Costanza was deliberately murdered."

"Good God!" The cigarette snapped in two.

"We hoped, as you once knew her very well, you might have some suggestion, some helpful clue, know of any enemies she might have made."

The unobtrusive man was back, bringing a tray with three glasses of iced coffee.

"I have not," Hendricks said distinctly, "had any communication with Dolores in at least fifteen years."

Cream slopped over the side of the pitcher and the bouncer-waiter murmured an apology as he wiped it up.

Hendricks waited until he had gone out of the room. "What are you trying to do?" he demanded, and it was not the ambassador speaking; it was a seasoned gambler calling for a show of cards.

Looking from one to the other, Judy thought that Hendricks would not be able to read much in Jon's face. Her own expression was so wide-eyed in its simplicity that Jon bit his lips and looked away until he could control the laugh in his throat.

"I—well, of course," she said, "Mrs. Hendricks was pretty bitter about Miss Costanza. She felt that she was to blame for breaking up her marriage and she felt that Dolores had made a fool of you."

Jon swallowed hard and risked a look at Hendricks, whose face was turning purple.

"But," Judy went on brightly, "she couldn't help but be kind of pleased, because she said you had made a fool of Dolores. She said that Dolores tried to force your hand and make you marry her by divorcing her husband and announcing publicly her plans about you. And then you didn't marry her, after all."

Hendricks gave Judy a wry smile. "Women!" he said, and shook his head ruefully. "Poor Ellen! But I don't know why I say poor. I settled half a million on her when she divorced me." He laughed softly, looking at Jon in man-to-man understanding. "And a bargain at that. She was a cute little trick, but I was fifty when she was twenty and looked—and acted—fifteen. It didn't take long to find that I had outgrown my taste for lollipops."

"I take it," Jon said, "that you were never serious about marrying Dolores."

"I had had a bellyful of marriage," Hendricks said succinctly. "I haven't seen Dolores or heard of her in years, not until I read of her fatal accident. You say murder?"

"We say murder," Jon told him.

"Incredible. She was well past the age when she could arouse any violent feelings in men, what with that dyed hair and those scars. She was a ruin."

Jon shook his head without looking at Judy and she closed her lips on what she had been about to say. She found herself frowning at him. It was uncomfortable having a man know what was in her mind as soon as she did herself.

"Well, after all, sex jealousy isn't the only reason for murder," Jon said. "Not even the most frequent. There are other things: financial gain, revenge, fear of exposure—" He let the words hang in the air.

Hendricks looked at his watch, got up. "Sorry, I can't help you." He seemed about to shake hands, changed his mind. "Rogers here said something about the *Sentinel*. Are you planning to do a story on Dolores, drag out all that old dead stuff? Because if that's the idea, I'll call your managing editor and put a stop to it or clap a suit on the paper that will cripple it worse than the past three newspaper strikes put together. I am awaiting confirmation of my appointment as ambassador and I am in a sensitive position. I cannot afford any publicity at this time. I do not intend to have any."

"I do hope," Jon said, "it won't be necessary for you to take any such drastic steps. We are just doing background work, looking up Miss Costanza's former associates, for one thing."

"Why don't you try her ex-husband? He was crazy about her. Might have kept in touch, though, of course, she divorced him."

Jon took Judy's arm, steered her toward the door. He turned back to ask casually, "By the way, Miss Costanza never turned over to you a briefcase, did she?" They were watching each other like wrestlers now. "For safekeeping," he added gently.

Hendricks made no reply. He wheeled and went out of the room. The man called Rogers returned, held the door for them.

"I was wondering," Jon said quietly, "whether there have been any telephone messages lately for Mr. Hendricks from Miss Costanza?"

"You heard him, mister."

"But—"

The man edged forward, his arm pressed almost casually against Fullbright, thrusting him through the open doorway and into the corridor. "If you know what's good for you, get going."

"I'm good for fifty dollars," Fullbright said. He dropped his card on the carpet and followed Judy toward the elevators. Half turning, Judy saw the man Rogers bend to pick up the card, read it, pocket it. The door closed behind them.

II

"You know what?" Judy demanded when they were out on Park Avenue, the sidewalk so hot that it seemed to burn through the thin soles of her shoes. "I wouldn't be a bit surprised if that man was armed."

Jon laughed. "Neither would I."

"Hendricks is scared to death, isn't he? Afraid of publicity."

"Well, afraid of something, at any rate."

"You may not have noticed it, but he was lying about Costanza. The way he described her, that's the way she looked when I saw her, not the way she was in those old photographs."

"Yes, I noticed."

"Jon." She slipped her hand under his arm. "I think maybe he's the one." When he made no comment, her hand tightened on his arm. "Well? What do you think?"

"He's still on my list."

He wasn't going to add to that. After a moment Judy asked, "What do we do next?"

"Try the ex-husband, Elmer Burbank."

"You think he's the most important?"

"I think he's the nearest at hand. Madison Avenue, six blocks away. Can you walk it? There doesn't seem to be a cab in sight."

"Of course I can walk it." The day had become very dark, the air was like a smothering wet blanket over them. In the distance there was a rumble of thunder, hardly noticeable above the roar of motors and the sound of traffic. "I wish the storm would break."

"It will," he said, and at something in his voice Judy looked at him quickly.

"I'll bet," she said after devoting some time to this fruitless effort, "you are a demon at poker."

"I like a friendly game, but I'm careful about choosing the people I play with."

"You wouldn't play with Hendricks."

"Not until I'd made him shake out his sleeves."

Melcher and O'Brien occupied two floors of a big Madison Avenue building. There was thick carpeting in the reception room, a blonde in a mini skirt at the reception desk, deep chairs, modern paintings on the walls. There was a faint scent in the air, a discreet perfume, a sampling of one of the products they advertised.

Melcher and O'Brien were in the chips. Along the corridor behind the reception room, and shut off from it by a glass wall, there was a constant procession of messenger boys carrying files and looking hurried, of girls in mini skirts carrying notebooks and looking seductive, of sincere young men with dedicated faces and Brooks Brothers suits, looking harried.

Mr. Burbank had gone for the day, the receptionist said. Perhaps someone else, our Mr. Ford works closely with Mr. Burbank on some of the same accounts, or Mr. Burbank's secretary.

Elmer Burbank's secretary, unlike the receptionist and the trim stenographers, was a woman of fifty, conservatively dressed in a dark sheer sheath that covered her knees, her graying hair cut short, shrewd eyes behind bifocals. After some talk back and forth over the telephone the receptionist had called one of the young messengers and had him conduct them along the corridor, past offices whose furnishings indicated as clearly as army insignia the exact position of each person. This ranged from rooms with carved Italian desks and deep carpeting, draperies, flowers in vases and good paintings on the walls, to more modest rooms with two desks each, Venetian blinds at the windows, carpetless floors and wall decorations consisting of advertisements of various products, which ran the gamut from extra long cigarettes and floor waxes to the agency's speciality, soaps and soap products.

There was a splendid corner office which indicated the prestige of its occupant by having a completely bare desk, a fireplace, a couch, several big chairs, and, on the wall, an oil painting of a woman in evening dress, posed in imitation of the famous Sargent portrait. It was rather a cruel portrait because the woman's face was not memorable while the fabric of her evening dress and the matched pearls that hung to her waist in a double strand were fabulous.

There was a small plaque on the open door of this empty room indicating that it was the domain of Elmer Burbank. Jon blinked in surprise. Apparently Elmer Burbank was no mere account executive—he was the real head of Melcher and O'Brien.

Elmer Burbank's secretary occupied the next office, a small businesslike room with a desk, filing cases, three telephones, and a typewriter. On the wall there was an oil painting of a hard-looking man with pouches under his eyes, a thick nose, and an expression that indicated he suffered from chronic indigestion.

The secretary got up to meet them and shook hands in a firm, no-nonsense manner. "I am Mr. Burbank's secretary, Helen Goody. Miss Goody." She stressed the Miss slightly.

"I am Jonathan Fullbright. This is Miss Wilkins."

She looked them over, indicated chairs, sat at her desk, erect, businesslike. "What can I do to help you?"

"I'm not sure," Jon admitted. "Actually we are here on personal business." He broke off to look at the portrait.

The woman's face brightened, warmed. "That was

John Wellington, who founded the Super-suds Company. I was his stenographer from the time I was sixteen, and his secretary until he died."

"In times like these, that is a marvelous record of loyalty," Jon said.

"On both sides," she told him. "As Mr. Wellington went up and his business grew, he took all us old-timers along with him, just as far as we could go. And he left us all comfortably pensioned so that we could retire without scrimping."

"But you are the kind who prefers to work."

"Well, I was devoted to the whole family. And when his only child, his daughter Hazel, married, she put quite a bit of money into Melcher and O'Brien—"

"In fact, controlling stock."

Miss Goody nodded. "She wanted to create a position in which her husband, Mr. Burbank, could do full justice to his talents and enjoy his work. And she arranged for him to bring the Super-suds account with him." Her voice was flat and expressionless.

She doesn't like him at all, Judy thought, and was about to speak when she felt once more that Jon was willing her to be silent.

Jon did not look at her. He smiled at Miss Goody. "And Mrs. Burbank not only provided her husband with a flourishing business but with a—faithful secretary."

Miss Goody looked up, looked down at a pencil which seemed to obsess her as she twirled it between her fingers. "You might say so."

And there it was. Hazel Wellington Burbank was infatuated with her husband, but she did not trust him an inch. Neither did the faithful secretary. Judy, engrossed in wondering how Miss Goody managed to report to her real employer without indicating that either of them was aware of what she was about, lost track of the conversation. She came back with a start when she heard Jon say, "I suppose you have seen the newspaper account of the death of Miss Dolores Costanza a few days ago."

Miss Goody held tight to the pencil, turned it over and over. "Yes, I saw it."

"You know, of course, that she was Mr. Burbank's first wife."

"Yes, of course."

"I don't suppose you would be likely to know—that is, we are trying to find anyone who saw Miss Costanza shortly before her death."

"Why?" Miss Goody was not one to waste words.

"Because it seems probable that she was murdered and that her killer has destroyed at least one other life and endangers a third."

The pencil broke with a snap and she threw it into the wastebasket. "That's horrible," she said at last. "Really horrible. She wasn't a good person at all, so far as I can make out, but she didn't deserve that. And to think of such a killer being loose. It's—just awful."

"I suppose you didn't know her at all. Miss Costanza dropped out of her profession shortly after the divorce, as I understand it."

Miss Goody was thoughtful. Then she said, "Actually, I not only saw her, I talked with her quite recently. Not more than a week ago."

"Where was that?"

"Here at the office. I was just returning from lunch one day and she was at the reception desk asking about possible employment, doing commercials for some of our clients. We had a new receptionist at the time who was not certain where to send her. I talked to her for a few minutes, realized that while she had an excellent speaking voice and a mobile face—well, that is, you know what's needed for these things, a look of great surprise or great distress. For some reason, people must constantly be astounded by advertising messages. But she wasn't up to our standards."

"You think she had come here to ask her ex-husband for a job?"

"No, that's the odd part of it. She didn't know of his position here; all she knew were the names of our leading accounts."

"Are you sure of that?"

"Quite sure. Mr. Burbank had an early afternoon appointment and he came back early. I don't think he even recognized her. He nodded to me, asked a question, and started on through the reception room and she said, in that clear, carrying voice of hers, 'Why, Elmer darling!'"

"After a long moment he had replied, 'Doris! I didn't know you.'

"'I've changed a lot. You don't need to tell me. But you seem to be flourishing.'

"'Well, thanks. Nice to have seen you.' He tried to escape, but she caught hold of his arm.

"When he realized the receptionist and I were watching," Miss Goody went on, "he took her back to his office. I heard her say, 'My, you do yourself well, my pet! It wasn't like that in the old days. Who's the pinup?' And he said, 'My wife.' She began to laugh and he closed the door."

"That's all?" Jon asked.

"That's all. She was there only about fifteen minutes. Mr. Burbank had an important appointment. I never saw or heard of her again."

"Did she," Jon asked, "have a briefcase with her?"

For the first time Miss Goody was uncertain. "I don't know. If she did, it made no impression on me."

"And that was the last of her so far as you are concerned?"

"Well, she spoke to someone on her way down the hall. I heard her exclaim, 'Good God, this is certainly Old Home Week! I didn't know you at first, Hugh, behind all that hair. Why hide a beautiful face behind a beard like that?'"

"Hugh! Do you know whom she was talking to?"

Miss Goody shook her head. "I was busy. I'd have had to go out in the corridor and it didn't matter."

"Did you ever hear of a man named Hugh Allison?"

Another shake.

"Is there anyone around here who hides a beautiful face behind a lot of hair and a big beard?"

"Well, there's Bill Bennett who does a series of true crime dramas, sponsored by one of our accounts. Actually, it is Super-suds. You must have seen the program. It has won several awards. Bill has a big beard that pretty much covers his face. How beautiful he is without it," and her voice was dry, "I have no idea."

"And where does Bill Bennett hang out?"

Miss Goody raised her eyebrows, seemed about to protest, and then lifted the telephone. She got an address on Riverside Drive.

"You have been very helpful, Miss Goody."

"If you are trying to run down a murderer, I hope you aren't after Bill Bennett. He is really good, he does prestige stuff, and he keeps up his standards. I wouldn't like to see anything happen to him."

"Would you," Jon asked, "regard him as a violent man?"

Miss Goody got up to take leave of them. She smiled slightly. "Who isn't? There are times when I feel murderous myself. Good afternoon, Mr. Fullbright. Miss Wilkins."

Jon grinned at her. "Don't give too bad a report to Mrs. Burbank."

Unexpectedly she grinned back at him with a look of amused complicity. "You'll have nothing to complain of."

10

The Hudson was dark, leaden, a sullen and turgid river. A few freighters were at anchor on the Jersey side. In the distance, against a lowering sky, the George Washington Bridge's two levels revealed antlike shapes that were cars moving across in an endless stream.

The apartment building was old-fashioned, with an impressive lobby with a marble floor, plush chairs that belonged to nineteen hundred, and an elaborate chandelier.

There was no doorman and the young man at the switchboard raised inquiring eyes from the book he was reading. As an inveterate reader, Jon instinctively craned his head to see the title, Edith Hamilton's *The Roman Way*.

"Wonderful book, isn't it?"

"Well," the reader said thoughtfully, "it's discouraging to see how little we improve in a thousand years."

Jon laughed. "You've got a point. Is Mr. Bennett in?"

"He went out a couple of hours ago, but he may have come back. The elevator's self-service now and I might not have noticed him if he didn't speak." He plugged in, rang, finally shook his head.

"I don't suppose you have any idea where I could find him."

The man at the switchboard hesitated. "Sometimes, when his stories get stuck, he goes to Jake's Bar over on Broadway. He's been out a lot the last few days. I don't know. Shall I take a message?"

Jon thought about it. "Actually I don't know where he could reach me. I'll have to call him."

"May I have your name?"

"I doubt if he would know it. Fullbright. Jonathan Fullbright."

The eyes of the man at the switchboard were more alert, interested. *"Such Men Are Dangerous?"*

Jon grinned, half surprised, half flattered.

"That's a fine book, Mr. Fullbright. I nearly wrote you about it when I finished it, but I figured you wouldn't want to be bothered."

"You couldn't have been more mistaken. I'd like to know what you think."

"Then I'll get it all down on paper one of these days." The man at the switchboard shook Jon's outstretched hand. "I hope you're doing another."

"Like Mr. Bennett, I seem to have struck a snag."

A gust of hot wind, always one of the least pleasant features of Riverside Drive, drove dust into Judy's eyes, swirled a piece of newspaper around one ankle, rattled the raincoat under her arm.

"Where next?" she asked.

"I was just debating. I'm going over to Jake's Bar to see whether I can round up this Bennett-Allison character. Why don't you plan to meet me in the waiting room at Grand Central? We can pick up your suitcases there."

She tucked her hand firmly under his arm. "I am not going to be left out at this point."

"Look here, Judy, fun is fun, but this guy has the strongest motive of anyone we've heard of so far. If he's our man, he has already killed two women, and he tried to kill you. Next time—" He saw her expression and heaved a loud, exasperated sigh. "Come on, wench, but don't say I didn't warn you."

They went up the street, across West End Avenue, up a steeper street to Broadway. There was a subway kiosk on the corner, a delicatessen smelling of dill pickles and cheese, a shoeshine parlor, a small shop whose window was filled with transparent black underwear at which Judy stared in astonishment. Jake's Bar was unexpectedly well lighted, it had booths along one side, there was no juke box in operation, and the bartender, the only person in sight, was busy polishing brass. He turned around to smile a greeting. Though there was no air conditioning, the place was comfortably cool after the relentless baking heat of the street.

"Hot enough for you?" he asked cheerfully.

Before Jon could answer, a man's voice from a booth at the back said irritably, "For God's sake, Jake, stop saying that! It wasn't funny when the first fool said it a thousand years ago. It gets less funny all the time." The voice was rather blurred.

Jake shrugged, grinned at the newcomers. "What'll it be, folks?"

"Gin and tonic all right?" Jon asked, and Judy nodded. "With lime." He led her casually past the empty booths, paused at the one that was occupied.

He was a very hairy man indeed, and he was very drunk. Jon's hand tightened on Judy's arm and he stepped forward, casually interposing his body between her and the man in the booth.

"Hello, Allison," he said carefully. "Where have you been keeping yourself?"

"Who are you?" The man's eyes were bloodshot. He had a big fan-shaped beard and whiskers that covered his cheeks. Only the red-veined eyes and the beautifully shaped straight nose were uncovered by that mass of hair.

"My name is Fullbright."

"I hope," the drunk said, "you find that information more interesting than I do." His voice rose in a roar. "Jake, throw this guy out! I come here for peace and privacy."

"You come here," Fullbright said, "to get stewed to the gills, don't you, Hugh?"

"I come here," the drunk said with elaborate dignity, "when the well runs dry, when inspiration fades, when I find myself—"

"Nuts!"

"Then why do you think I come?" The drunk leaned forward, watching Fullbright's face as though challenging him. "How do you solve this fash—fascinating enigma?"

"You've been drowning your sorrows in here for several days, haven't you, Hugh?"

"Name's Bill. Bill Bennett. Creator of *How It Happened* series. Mosh brilliant—authentic—crime stories, mosh—but a guy gets tired."

"Where do you get your material, Hugh?"

"Name's—"

"I know your name. It was Hugh Allison until you went to prison." Beside him, the bartender, holding two tall glasses, sucked in his breath and edged away, back to the bar counter. Jon signaled him and ordered black coffee.

The man peered at him, trying to focus. "Go 'way."

"Why?" Jon took the coffee from the bartender, put it in front of Allison and edged his shot glass of whiskey out of reach.

"Let the pash bury its dead."

"Only it won't do that, will it, Hugh? It keeps coming back, the way Dolores came back."

"She laughed," Hugh Allison said thickly. Automatically he began to drink the coffee, appearing to be rather surprised when he tasted it. "She looked at me and she laughed. All that hair on my beautiful face, she said. She laughed. She was going to tell Burbank who I was. Advertising is a very shen—sensitive industry. They wouldn't hire an ex-convict. Not if they knew. She smashed my whole life. I dipped in the till —you knew that?"

Jon nodded, still standing carefully between Judy and the drunk.

"She wanted diamonds. She was crazy for diamonds. And she said Hendricks would get them for her if I didn't. So I land in prison. Well, that is when Hugh Allison died. No more banking. I taught myself to write while I was there. I had a crazy idea I could write the whole story and clear myself in a way. Show people what she really was like. Then when I came out, it didn't matter much."

"You mean you'd forgiven her?"

Allison laughed. "I hated her guts. She could at least have helped me make restitution, but she wouldn't give up the earrings. I hated her guts. The way she died—too good for her. A few seconds and it was all over. I had three years in the pen, and all these years I've hidden behind this damned hair. I built a new life, better than I'd had before except—no more women." He waved his hand solemnly in a gesture of rejection. "No—more—women."

"And then she showed up at Melcher and O'Brien."

"She ran into Burbank. You know what he and I are?" His eyes screwed up and he looked wisely at Jon. He nodded his head emphatically. "Brothers under the skin. That's what. Brothers under the skin." He began to laugh in a choking sort of way.

"Did Miss Costanza mention a briefcase to you?"

The fingers that were fumbling in their effort to draw a cigarette out of a package he held clamped tightly in the other hand gave up their fruitless effort. He half rose, his hand closing around the coffee cup. Jon shoved Judy out of the way as the cup struck against the far side of the booth and the hot liquid splashed over the wall and the seat.

Jake moved then. Jon put down the money for the drinks and steered Judy toward the door. Jake waited until they had hailed a cab and climbed in before he hoisted Hugh Allison to his feet.

"Okay, boy," he said soothingly. "Okay. Take it easy. We're just going along now. You've had a snootful." He eased him out of the door and stared after him. Like Jon, he was aware of the latent danger in the man. He watched in relief as he staggered across the street, heading in an uneven course down the hill toward Riverside Drive.

II

There was a streak of lightning, followed almost immediately by a heavy rumble of thunder, and then the storm broke with a heavy rush of rain that swept down the highway, pouring like waves over the windshield so that the wipers could not keep pace.

Jon pulled off the Saw Mill Parkway into the first emergency parking space and settled back, relaxed, waiting for visibility to be restored. He seemed to be in no hurry at all. Beside him, Judy watched the storm, the rush of rain that was already filling gutters, hearing the thunder, starting in spite of herself at the lightning flashes. Without looking at her, Jon reached out and took her hand, holding it in his own, and gradually her tremors stopped.

The first fury of the storm exhausted itself, the lightning ceased, the thunder was only a distant sound as the storm disappeared over the city, headed for Brooklyn. The rain eased off, though it still drummed steadily on the roof of the car, and as the wind died down, Judy risked opening the side vent and felt the air, cool and sweet, fresh and reviving on her face.

Behind her were the two suitcases which they had collected at Grand Central Station. Ahead—but she had no idea what was ahead, which was par for the course of the past two days. At the moment she did not even want to ask. Something in the repressed violence of Hugh Allison had terrified her, or would have terrified her if Jon had not been there, had not been a shield between her and any form of violence.

"He could have killed her and Peg," she said at last. "He could be the one who came up the fire escape."

"Yes," Jon agreed. He did not seem to have anything else to contribute.

"Where are we going next?"

"To see the rest of the cast, Mr. and Mrs. Elmer Burbank."

"We don't even know that they are the rest of the cast. There may be more."

"So there may," he agreed placidly, "but according to the program I hold, that's the cast."

"And if there is someone else, and there may be any number of people, people we've never heard of, what will we do then?"

"Keep on digging."

"And if we don't find anyone, what then? Do I just wait for the murderer to catch up with me?"

If he heard the quaver in her voice, he gave no indication of it. "If we don't find anyone, then we'll have to smoke him out."

"Smoke him out how?" She was sitting upright, staring at him suspiciously.

"I have no idea, but it's a sort of last resort."

She thought about it. "If he thinks I have the briefcase, then there's only one last resort I can see, and that is to make me the cheese in the mousetrap."

"If I set any trap with you as bait, I'll be waiting right at the mousehole," he told her.

"Maybe you could record my last words," she said morosely.

He started the car without replying and slid back into traffic. There was no sound but the rhythmic swish of the windshield wipers, the drumming of rain on the roof, the sudden blare of a radio in a passing car.

By the time they had left the highway, turned onto a secondary, tree-lined road, and approached a high evergreen wall, the rain had dropped to a trickle.

The name Burbank was on a mailbox on one side of the road; on the other side open gates bore the name Elmer Burbank on one pillar and Wellon Manor on the other.

"Good God!" Jon ejaculated. "Manor yet."

"I've seen pictures of the place in one of those big magazines. It belonged to John Wellington, the head of a soap company. His daughter inherited it. There was a double spread in color, showing the grounds with the swimming pool, stables, tennis court and rose gardens. It's fantastic."

Jon grunted, followed a circular sweep up past a beautifully kept lawn, flower beds, big trees, to the front of a long gray-stone Palladian house.

"Need your raincoat?"

"Not now."

Before Judy could open the door on her side, a man ran lightly down the broad shallow flight of stairs from the entrance and opened the door for her.

"I am Miss Wilkins. Is Mrs. Burbank at home?"

Jon came around the car and the man reached for his car keys. "I'll park for you, sir." He led the way up the steps and into a long baronial hall that seemed more appropriate for some English estate of the vanished past than for a suburban home of today. He caught the eye of a passing maid. "Miss Wilkins and—"

"Jonathan Fullbright."

The maid led the way past a formal drawing room, which appeared to have a number of French impressionistic paintings, past a smaller room with red draperies, black leather chairs, a desk, and a couple of shelves of books, probably known as a den, and down a couple of steps into an unexpectedly dramatic room with two glass walls, which extended toward the garden and seemed almost a part of it. Doors rolled open onto a terrace with bright lawn chairs, tables, umbrellas, and a stunning arrangement of plants and flowers.

The woman who rose to greet them was, somehow, as diminished by her surroundings as she had been diminished in the oil painting by her jewelry. She was a young and healthy forty, with a clear skin browned by hours out of doors, her hair beautifully arranged, her simple summer dress a Dior creation.

"Miss Wilkins?" She had a warm handshake and a radiant smile. "Mr. Fullbright. Do sit down and make yourselves comfortable. Tea? A cocktail? A long drink? What would you prefer?"

"Nothing at all, thank you." Jon spoke for both of

them. "We are awfully sorry to intrude in this way, but the fact is—"

She helped him out, smiling. "I know. Dear old Goody called me. She thought you would be coming up here. I suppose really it is Elmer you should see, but he has been delayed by the storm. He was playing golf with an executive for one of his accounts and I suppose they just holed up somewhere when it began to rain. At least I hope so. Otherwise they will be soaked. I do think summer colds are a pest, don't you? So hard to shake off." She seemed prepared to continue this gentle flow of aimless talk indefinitely, but she broke off to smile at two youngsters who had paused in the doorway.

"These," she said brightly, "are my jewels, Elmer junior and Helen." The boy was about twelve and trim in riding clothes. The girl was probably nine, rather plain but with her mother's pleasant face, firm chin, and direct eyes. She curtseyed and the boy said, "Hi. That is, how do you do?"

"Later, children." Mrs. Burbank dismissed them with a cheerful nod and they went without protest or delay. The iron hand couldn't have had a softer glove, Jon reflected.

"I suppose Miss Goody told you why we are making such a nuisance of ourselves."

"Not at all," Mrs. Burbank said politely. "Goody mentioned that you were asking about my husband's first wife. That poor woman! What a ghastly way to die! A dreadful thing. I never knew her myself, but I suppose," and she smiled disarmingly at Judy, "I always rather resented her. Even though she belonged to the past she was, in a way, a kind of competition. All that glamour. But to die so horribly—" She shook her head in what appeared to be real distress.

Judy realized with a kind of shock that Mrs. Burbank was watching them both closely. She wasn't altogether the simple person she appeared at first glance.

"Murder is always horrible," Jon said.

"That's what Goody told me, that you thought she

had been murdered, but you must be mistaken. Why would anyone do that? It's so long since she was really important to anyone."

"There has to be so powerful a reason that it led someone not only to kill her but to kill another woman in an attempt to destroy some evidence against him, and then to attempt to kill a third."

"Could it be—well, someone who hates women? Like Jack the Ripper? Something like that?"

Jon shook his head. "About all we are sure of is that Dolores Costanza, when she couldn't earn money any other way, turned blackmailer. She had made an appointment with the managing editor of the *Sentinel* to see him the day after she was killed. She was going, she told him, to blow things sky-high."

"So in a way she really was asking for it." Mrs. Burbank's unexpectedly intelligent eyes met Jon's. "I don't want to waste your time, so I must state quite directly and clearly that Miss Costanza never approached me in her life, that she never attempted to blackmail me. And she couldn't have done it. One thing I learned from my father was that it is a mistake to let anyone bluff you."

"You know," Jon agreed, "that's what I thought when I first saw you. Oh, by the way, I understand you know Mrs. Hendricks, Ellen Wills Hendricks, whose marriage was broken up by the—uh—former Mrs. Burbank."

"Why, yes. At least we play bridge now and then and occasionally lunch together. We are both ardent bridge players. But surely you don't suspect Ellen of violence!" She laughed at the absurdity of the idea. "She is really a very sensible person in spite of her childish ways. And I find it interesting to meet someone and then see them in one of those old movies. Makes it more interesting to know what they're like in real life."

"Do you know Mr. Hendricks?"

"No, they were divorced years ago, before I even met Elmer, and I've known her only recently. I understand the President has put up his name for an ambassadorial post." Her voice quickened. "But would he still have a grudge against Doris—uh, Dolores Costanza?"

"I have no idea."

"From what Ellen says, I always imagined Mr. Hendricks as being rather stodgy."

"Whoever killed Dolores was afraid of exposure of some kind. That's about all we can be sure of. Nearly anyone has something in his background he would hate to have made public. Don't you agree?"

"I suppose so. But I can tell you this, Mr. Fullbright, there is nothing like that in my husband's life. Absolutely nothing. Just the same, the slightest threat of bad publicity would be awful. Advertising is a sensitive business, Mr. Fullbright. Very sensitive. Especially since the late Senator Joseph McCarthy simply strewed suspicions around."

"So I understand. Do you happen to know whether your husband met his former wife recently?"

"What the hell!" The man who came into the room, still in golfing clothes, a raincoat slung over his shoulders, was big and virile, good-looking in a rough-hewn sort of way, and at the moment he was in a towering temper. "What goes on here?"

"This is my husband," Mrs. Burbank said. Her voice was quiet and soothing. "Miss Wilkins. Mr. Fullbright. These nice young people are looking into the death of your—of Doris. They," and there was a hint of warning in her voice, "have just come from the office, where they talked to dear old Goody."

Burbank was a quick man to take a hint. The scowl left his face. He shook hands with them, automatically giving Judy a quick approving once-over.

"Yes, well, the poor old girl. I suppose Goody told you that, after all these years, Doris came to the office the other day. Didn't even know I worked there. Trying all the agencies, I suppose, looking for a job doing commercials." He shook his head. "I'll tell you the truth," he said confidentially, "I didn't even recognize her. If ever a woman had fallen apart at the seams, she had."

"I hope, Elmer," his wife led him deftly, "you were able to do something for the poor thing."

"Well, we couldn't use her, not the way she looked. And, to tell you the truth, I wouldn't have wanted to anyhow. It was pretty obvious that she had been hitting the bottle, and we don't want people like that. We don't want the word to go around. It's a sensitive business, you know." He shook his head. "Very sensitive."

"So I understand."

"But I gave her a little cash, maybe fifty dollars, whatever I happened to have on hand. Only I made clear that there wasn't any more where that came from. After all, she divorced me of her own free will a long time ago. There's no going back to the not-so-good old days, if you know what I mean."

Jon agreed that he knew what he meant.

"So how can we help you, Helen and I?" He went to slip his arm around his wife's shoulders.

"Dolores Costanza was murdered. We are looking for a motive."

Burbank looked as though the breath had been knocked out of him by a blow to the solar plexus. It took a full minute for him to say, "Have you found anything?"

"So far we've found Bill Bennett."

Burbank stiffened. "Bennett? Our true-crime man? Damn it, he's a valuable property. Keep off him. And I know you're mistaken; I know for a fact he has no part in women. He hates them. You're on the wrong track."

"Your ex-wife is the reason he hates women. He went to prison for stealing from his bank to buy her diamonds. His real name is Hugh Allison. He served three years and that is where he got his authentic material for his television plays."

Burbank blinked. "I'll be damned. I will be damned! Must have been those earrings. I thought they came from Hendricks. Look, Fullbright, Bennett—or whatever his name is—is good. He is tops. There must be some way to keep him in the clear on this."

"I don't say he killed Dolores," Jon said.

"Then who else?" Burbank's expression changed. This was the angry bull of a man who had come charging into the room in the first place.

"We have a few promising candidates. There's the man Hendricks."

"Well! Gordon Hendricks!" Burbank began to smile. "Well! You're breaking my heart."

"So I see."

"He took Doris away and flaunted the situation right in front of my eyes."

"If you can think of anything helpful." Jon glanced at Judy, collecting her, she thought indignantly, as though he were picking up his hat from a checking girl.

"I'll let you know. Sure." Jon stopped at the door. "Oh, by the way, was Dolores carrying a briefcase when you met her?"

Burbank gave his wife an absent-minded squeeze. "Take care of it, will you, honey? I got soaked on the golf course and I want to shower and change. Nice to have seen you both." He went out of the room.

"There really isn't anything else," Jon told Mrs. Burbank.

When the car door had been shut on Judy and Jon had rolled down the circular driveway to the road, she said, "Well, we've seen the whole cast, but we still don't know the plot."

"Speak for yourself. I think at this point I could probably write the script. That's not what is worrying me right now."

"What does?"

"What," he demanded, "what the sweet hell am I going to do about you tonight?"

11

The inn had succeeded in combining the best of two worlds. It had old-world atmosphere and charm as well as new-world comfort, which meant, in particular, air conditioning. It also, Jon assured Judy, had the best cook in Westchester County.

Apparently he was well known there, because the headwaiter, who had just turned away a party because of lack of space, beamed at him and found a table beside a window.

"Oh, look!" Judy cried, and Jon followed her enraptured eyes. Across the lawn from horizon to horizon there arched a rainbow.

Only when it had faded did she draw a long breath of sheer satisfaction and turn to find Jon looking at her. Something in his expression accelerated her heartbeat.

"That is supposed to be a sign of good luck, isn't it?" she asked.

"We could use some."

"But I thought you were sure, that you knew which one it is."

"Knowing and proving are different things." For the first time he had no trace of his usual assurance. He seemed to be at a loss.

"Aren't you going to tell me?"

"I don't dare. Your expression might as well be a mirror of your mind. Anyone looking at you would know exactly what you are thinking."

There was a moment's pause and then slowly, painfully, inexorably, color mounted in Judy's cheeks, burned in her forehead, flushed her throat with heat. And there wasn't a thing she could do to prevent it. She sat with her eyes glued to the menu and wished the earth would open up and swallow her.

"What will you have to start?" Jon asked, his voice impersonal, his own attention seeming to be preoccupied by the menu. "The lobster bisque is good here."

When the waiter had gone, she met his eyes at last, fear stronger than her self-consciousness. "Jon, I've got to know; I've simply got to."

"You've seen them all, Judy. You've heard everything I've heard. Which is your choice?"

She counted them on her fingers, as she said, in the order of their appearance: "Mrs. Collins, Maxwell Allington, Ellen Hendricks, Gordon Hendricks, Hugh Allison, Mrs. Burbank, Elmer Burbank."

After a moment she decided, "We can eliminate all the women, because it wasn't a woman who spoke on the telephone or who waited at the drugstore to get the briefcase or who tripped you up in your room and escaped down a fire escape."

"How about the telephone voice?"

She shook her head. "He must have changed it in some way, because it didn't sound like anyone we've met." She tasted lobster bisque, looked up in pleased surprise, and then gave it all her attention.

"Of course," she said thoughtfully, when the waiter had removed soup plates, "the one who could change his voice most easily would be Maxwell. Jon, do you think there's any connection there? Maxwell and Dolores and the Allison man and Mr. Burbank all have some association with television."

"I think that's what eventually brought them together again, but that is all."

"But all we really know is that Dolores had something on each of them, some sort of leverage. Apparently, as long as advertising is—"

"Use the word sensitive and I will not be answerable for the consequences," Jon warned her.

"I know. They're awfully frightened people, aren't

they? Both arrogant and insecure. And I don't suppose it matters really which one had the strongest motive from our standpoint. Things look different sizes to different people. They all felt they had something to lose and I suppose, when it comes right down to it, Maxwell's routine job is just as important to him as the post of ambassador to Hendricks. So it's really what kind of people they are, isn't it?"

She tasted veal scallopini in its rich brown gravy flavored with Madeira and sighed voluptuously. "Do you eat as well as this all the time? I should think you'd be about thirty pounds overweight."

"Restraint and self-control are my watchwords," he told her smugly.

He seemed to enjoy her enjoyment of the food but he himself was not hungry. He crumpled a roll, pushed around the food, apparently not in a mood for talk, so Judy went back to the problem: Maxwell, Gordon Hendricks, Hugh Allison, Elmer Burbank. Which one? Which of them had pushed Dolores Costanza in front of a subway train and bashed Peg over the head and held a pillow over Judy's face?

Maxwell did not seem to be a violent man, but he had been frightened. A cornered rat might be as dangerous as a treed cougar. Hendricks had appeared to be suave, under control, but he had lied about seeing Costanza. He was a gambler and the kind of gambler whom Jon wouldn't trust. A man who took chances against heavy odds? Judy shook her head, putting aside the problem of Hendricks.

Hugh Allison had the strongest cause for bitterness, and she had felt the latent menace in him as she had felt the approaching electric storm before it struck. And he was drinking himself silly. Trying to forget what he had done? Getting Dutch courage for what remained to be done?

Elmer Burbank had, so far as Judy could see, no particular reason to resent his former wife. The divorce had brought him nothing but good: a devoted wife instead of an unfaithful one, nice healthy children, a guaranteed income and high position and magnificent home.

One thing was sure. Helen Wellington Burbank was in love with her husband, but she was not one to be easily fooled. One misstep and Burbank would find himself out on his ear. And he wasn't, Judy thought, the kind of idiot who would risk his pleasant life by going out on a limb over another woman, though he obviously was not in love with his wife. He had probably learned all he needed to know about glamour girls from his first wife, and he seemed to be a sensible man who was aware of his good luck in being where he was.

Fullbright signed the check and took Judy back to the car. Several people in the restaurant spoke to him on his way out.

"You must be the local celebrity," Judy commented.

He laughed. "Most people know me here because I'm an old-timer. I still live in the house my great-grandfather built, and a lot of my neighbors have been around a long time, too."

He closed the door on her side and went around to slide into the driver's seat.

"What are we going to do now?" Judy asked in a small voice.

He addressed the wheel. "I'm taking you home. It's the best I can think of for the night. I considered checking you in at the inn, but I remember staying there once when the house was being redecorated. Anyone could break those flimsy locks and there's no night clerk, no one on the lookout for sneak thieves or anything like that. You'll be safe in my house. For tonight, at least."

"But this can't go on, can it?"

"No," Jon admitted, "it can't go on."

"And I'll never be safe until we find the briefcase. When I think I had it in my hand, that I could have found out what was in it—"

"That was my fault, my bad advice."

"I didn't have to take it. Anyhow, you've performed services over and beyond the call of duty ever since," Judy assured him. "There's no point in being wise after the event."

Unexpectedly the car braked, made a sharp turn onto an unmarked dirt road. The woods were so thick that the road was only a gash through the trees, not noticeable until one was opposite it. Under the arching trees, it was nearly dark and Jon switched on the headlights so they appeared to be moving through a tunnel.

With equal abruptness, the road made another sharp turn, came out on a quiet pool, willow-fringed, with lily pads floating on it. A buck, up to its belly in water, nibbled at the lilies. Jon shut off the motor and they watched until the buck walked gravely away into the woods. Then Judy saw the house beyond a deep velvety lawn, a big stone house with an old-fashioned turret at one corner, making it look in the gathering darkness like an old castle.

"I'll take you in the back way if you don't mind," he said. The driveway skirted the house. At the back, past a vegetable garden, there was an ugly old structure. "Used to be a stable, but my father had it converted into a three-car garage. Actually it now houses this Plymouth of mine, a surrey with the fringe on top and a sleigh which go back to a more leisurely age, and garden tools, lawn mowers, that sort of thing."

When he had garaged the car, he reached for her hand. "You won't be able to see the path; I should keep a flashlight in the car, but I know the place as I do my own hand." He led her through the garden and unlocked the kitchen door, switched on lights. After a long moment he began to laugh. "It gets everyone."

"I don't believe it. Do you mean you actually cook here?"

The kitchen was immense, with a fireplace in which an ox could have been roasted, settles on either side, an iron crane, copper pans on the walls. There was a rag rug on the floor with its wide polished boards, and open cupboards holding pewter plates, willow pattern dishes, milk glass, and Paul Revere silver.

"It's an antique collector's paradise," Judy said at last.

"We have a family rule: all antique collectors are shot when we see the whites of their eyes. However, this is strictly a display piece. We've been threatening for years to do something about it, but an early Fullbright," he grinned at the colonial furnishings, "not that early, of course, designed the place and collected the things. I suppose this room will stay as it is until the house is torn down."

"But why," Judy asked in dismay, "should the house be torn down?"

"It's too big for one person. Not practical. Hard as the devil to heat adequately in winter, and anyhow I rattle around in all this space. There's a woman who comes in daily to clean up, wash dishes, make beds, all that, but I'm a hermit when I am here—I have to be to get the work done—and I don't entertain except at the inn or in town so—well, it just isn't practical. However, the place isn't all period piece, of course. Come along."

He showed her a small but modern electrified kitchen and led the way into the other downstairs rooms: drawing room, library, dining room, a small card-room. Judy noticed that while he continued to chat lightly he was checking the fastening of every window and testing the locks and bolts on the doors.

The stairs rose in a lovely curve to the second floor. "A few modern improvements," Jon said. "The outdoor john was replaced by a single bathroom shared by the whole family. But as all the bedrooms had closets about as big as the rooms, we converted them into bathrooms. There are some advantages, after all, in getting out of period."

He opened a door. "There's no bedding, but I'll bring you some." He came back from a large closet carrying pillows, sheets, and blankets.

"I'll do this," Judy offered.

"Sure you can manage?"

"Of course."

"You'll be all right here. My room is across the hall in that tower affair. There's a winding staircase in the wall—I'll show you tomorrow—that leads up to my workroom. When I was a kid I thought that was the most romantic spot on earth. Well," he hesitated in the doorway. "Wait. I have an idea."

Judy heard him run down the stairs and in a few minutes he came back, triumphantly displaying a silver dinner bell. "I knew we had this somewhere. If anything—if you are nervous or anything, just ring that and I'll come running."

Judy set down the bell, staring at it. "And tomorrow night and the next one and the next one? Just waiting. How long is this going on?" Her voice was shrill, but she could not seem to control it.

"Look here," Jon said in alarm, "up to now you've been fine. You can't lose your nerve at this point."

She discovered that she was clinging to the lapels of his jacket, that she was shaking. His hands covered hers, then his arms went around her. He kissed her lightly, and then not lightly at all.

He released her so suddenly that his hands had to steady her when she staggered. Then he stepped back. "I warned you that I wouldn't be answerable for my intentions after one night. What we need here is a chaperon."

He touched her cheek with a fingertip. "All right, brat, go to bed and sleep well."

"Where are you going?" There was panic in her voice. It clutched at him as her hands might have done.

"I'm going to call up reinforcements." He laughed at her expression. "I'm going to telephone Lieutenant Krill and tell him what we've found out today and see if he can be persuaded to interest the State Police in keeping an eye on the house tonight."

12

It was the moon that kept Judy awake, a full moon that shone directly on her face. She lay staring at it, remembering how, the night before, it had been blotted out by a shadow, how someone had shoved a pillow over her face, shutting out the air. Maxwell? Hendricks? Allison? Burbank? She went over the possibilities. Which one? Which one?

This couldn't go on. Jon could not be expected to protect her indefinitely. Sooner or later, the man would catch her alone and defenseless. Tonight she understood more fully than she had before Dolores Costanza's terror.

She turned her head away from the window, pulled up a sheet to cover her face and shut out the moonlight. Then she jerked down the sheet again, remembering the pillow over her face.

You are turning into a neurotic, she told herself in anger, but it didn't help. She was scared silly. Anything was better than not knowing. If she could only know whom she had to fear! Jon knew; at least he believed he did. But knowing wasn't proof, he had said.

A telephone shrilled in the night and Judy found herself sitting bolt upright, her heart thudding. Across the hall a door opened and Jon ran downstairs. Apparently he had not been able to sleep either. Judy stole on tiptoe to her door.

"Hello . . . Hello . . . Who is this? . . . Hello." At length he put down the telephone and started up the stairs.

Judy opened the door of her bedroom a crack. "What was it?"

"You still awake? You aren't worrying, are you?"

"A bit. I can't help it. Who was that?"

"I don't know. Wrong number, maybe. Or someone playing games. No one answered."

"Maybe," she said in a small voice, "it was someone trying to find out if you were here."

"Well, then, he found out." Jon sounded cheerful and relaxed. If it hadn't been for the speed with which he had answered the telephone, Judy would have believed he was as unconcerned as he sounded. "Good night again." His door closed firmly.

Why, Judy wondered, would someone call and then not speak? Was it a good sign or a bad sign? Was the caller going to be scared away by Jon's presence in the house or was he going to be lured here by it? She started to get back in bed, saw the moonlight on her pillow, pulled up a big chair out of the light and sat facing the window. She would sit out the night there, on the lookout. She wouldn't let anyone creep up on her. Only, she knew bleakly, it couldn't go on this way. Sooner or later the intolerable situation had to end, whether for good or ill.

The moonlight shone on the pond where she had seen the buck nibbling at water lilies. Lights flickered in the woods beyond. Fireflies, she thought at first, but these were too big, too low, they never rose from their position near the ground. A car's parking lights coming closer. She was holding her breath now, straining to hear. There was the sound of wheels moving slowly over the graveled path. The sound stopped and the lights went out.

Then a long finger of light moved, following the driveway up to the house, leaped toward the bedroom windows. She was on her feet, groping for the bell. But she didn't want to warn the man outside. She pulled on a robe, ran across the hall, tapped on Jon's door.

"What is it?" he said, his voice alert, and she knew he had not been sleeping either.

"Jon, there is someone outside. I heard the car come up the driveway. Then the lights went out. Now there is someone walking around with a flashlight. He turned it on the driveway and then on the bedroom windows."

Jon's feet hit the floor and in a moment he opened his door. At what he saw in her face he pulled her into his arms, holding her tightly, her head pressed against his shoulder. "It's all right. I told you I was going to call Krill. I got hold of him and gave him a rundown on our interviews today and asked him to have the State Police up here keep an eye on the house tonight. They are probably just taking a look at the place. Don't worry, honey."

She drew away from him. "How do you know it's the police? How can you be sure?"

"Okay, I'll check up. You go back to your room."

"No." She clutched at his sleeve. "No, don't leave me here." As he went downstairs, she followed at his heels like a frightened small puppy, determined not to be left alone.

When he was halfway down the long lovely staircase, the doorbell rang and Judy stifled a gasp. She clung to Jon's sleeve, holding him back. "Don't open the door," she begged him. "Don't."

"You're being childish. You're all right, Judy. I keep telling you that."

He crossed the hall, switched on the outside lights and opened the door. For a moment the man outside was silhouetted sharply against the light. Then there was a sharp report that reverberated in the night and the man fell forward, the weight of his body throwing Jon off balance. For a moment he seemed to lean against Jon, and then he slid to his knees and crumpled at his feet.

Jon thrust Judy aside so forcefully that she fell back against a long table and set a lamp rocking. He turned off the outside lights, dragged the injured man inside, bolted the door, and then turned on the hall light, all in a matter of seconds. He stood looking down at the blood oozing from a hole in the man's coat. Gently he turned him over.

"It's Rogers," Judy exclaimed in astonishment. "The man from the Royal Flush Club. But why—I don't understand why he would come here."

"To collect the fifty dollars I promised him. But that isn't the point."

"Then what is?" Judy asked stupidly.

"Who is at the other end of that rifle and where is he? Get some hot water, will you, and some brandy. You'll find the liquor in that corner cupboard in the cardroom." His voice rose. "You little fool! Stay away from the windows. Don't you realize the man is probably still out there?"

He dialed a number. "Doctor, this is Fullbright. There has been an accident here. . . . He's been shot. . . . I don't know. I don't like moving him too much because he is bleeding a lot. I'm calling the police now."

He dialed again and said, "I want a policeman." He gave his name and address. "And tell them there is someone loose around here with a rifle. A man has been shot."

Afraid to move the injured man, Jon stuffed his handkerchief under his coat, trying to stanch the blood that kept seeping out. He took the brandy that Judy brought him and held it to the man's lips, lifting his head as little as possible, just enough so that he could swallow without choking.

Out on the highway there was a scream of brakes, a crash, shouts.

"Oh, God!" Judy exclaimed on a sob. Then she pulled herself together and knelt beside Rogers, her fingers groping for his pulse. The first attempt to get him to drink failed, and the brandy ran down his chin. The second time Jon managed to get a little in his mouth. The third time the man's throat moved as he swallowed. His eyes opened.

"The bastard shot me," he said thickly.

"Who shot you?" Jon asked.

"Hendricks, of course." Rogers closed his eyes and sagged back on the floor.

Jon got up to draw the shades and switch on the outside lights for the doctor. When the car pulled up before the house, he went to the side window, eased up the blind a trifle, and peered out. "It's the doctor."

Dr. Brenning was middle-aged, brisk, and at the moment disapproving. "Never know what hazards a doctor is going to run," he commented as he set down his bag and knelt beside the wounded man. "You'd better call the State Police."

"I did that right after I called you."

"That bunch is in a ditch down the pike. The police car turned over. And there had better be an ambulance. I stopped for a minute, but there was nothing serious that I could tell. Seemed to be mostly minor injuries. Still it is best to be sure. I must admit, after your call, I kept expecting someone to take a pot shot at me."

"I imagine this particular guy is selective," Jon told him. "He is after me or Miss Wilkins here. Or both."

The doctor looked Judy over in some surprise and gave Jon a sharp look. "Very young, isn't she?" His tone was disapproving.

"Too young to die," Jon said. "That's why she is here until some better form of protection can be set up for her and a killer is put permanently out of the way."

"We can do without the young lady for the time being," the doctor said, and Judy withdrew to the drawing room, where she stood in the dark, looking out on the moonlit lawn, wondering where the man Hendricks was. She was mildly surprised to realize that her teeth were chattering. However she might have appeared to herself in daydreams, there was no ignoring the shameful fact that she was a coward.

There was a murmur of voices from the hall, Rogers grunted as he was prodded, and then the doctor's voice rose, clear and concise. "No, we won't try to get him up those stairs if you have a couch of some kind handy on this floor. Or can bring down a mattress."

"Judy," Jon shouted, "get sheets for the davenport in there, will you, and a pillow."

She ran upstairs, grateful for something to do, foraged in the closet, ran down to make up a bed hastily on the davenport in the drawing room.

The two men came into the room, carrying Rogers between them, put him down carefully on the long davenport. His coat and shirt had been removed, and there was strapping over the ribs on his right side.

"Just a graze really," the doctor told Judy. "The bullet barely cut through the skin. He'll be all right. Bit of a shock, of course, and he's lost some blood. I'll see him again in the morning."

"I can't stay here," Rogers protested. "He'll get me for sure. I'm just a sitting duck."

"The State Police will be here soon," Jon assured him.

"Anyhow," the doctor said, "I'd take it for granted he won't be back here tonight."

"I won't take anything for granted," Jon said.

"I'm going now," the doctor told him. "Nothing more to do here. I'll take another look at the guys in the ditch. If you like, I'll send the ambulance back for this fellow."

"I like," Rogers said grimly.

"I'll have to report a bullet wound, you know."

"That's swell with me." Rogers was vicious.

When the doctor's car had gone, Jon came back to look down at the wounded man, who looked up at him intently.

"Okay, Rogers, what makes you think Hendricks tried to kill you tonight?"

"He lied to you about that Costanza woman," Rogers said. "She telephoned him at the Royal Flush three times. After the first time Hendricks instructed me to tell her he was not there. The last time she left a message. I wrote it down and I remember it word for word: 'You'll come to see me tomorrow or I'll come there and raise a noise they'll hear in Congress.' So after you left today, I—"

As he seemed to have difficulty in going on, Jon helped him out. "You put a bite on."

"Well—"

"Didn't get anywhere?"

"Hendricks knew I was bluffing, that I didn't really know the score. He said so. He just laughed and said, 'Try it.' So I figured he had outbluffed me and that I'd probably be fired for trying to put on the bite. And you had said you were good for a hundred bucks."

"Fifty."

Rogers grinned impudently. "And me with a hole in my ribs."

"You're lucky it wasn't a hole through your heart." Jon wasn't sympathetic.

In the distance there was the rise and fall of a siren. The top blinker of a police car could be seen in the woods. A few minutes later, the police car came up the driveway and Jon, after a sharp "Keep back" to Judy, went to open the door. Three men came into the room, at one of whom he looked in surprise.

"Well, well," Lieutenant Krill said, his mouth widening in a smile like an alligator's, "I do meet you under the most amazing circumstances, Miss Wilkins." He looked at Jon. "I decided to come up here after the Westchester police said you had called. I figured you might be up to something."

"Someone was," Jon said.

Judy pulled her robe more closely around her. She could feel the color burning in her cheeks, but she held her head high. 'Mr. Fullbright has been kind enough to afford me the protection that the police has failed to give me, Lieutenant."

The man beside Krill swallowed and tried to look blank.

"Miss Wilkins," Krill said, "this is Lieutenant

Graves of the Westchester police and Sergeant King. Mr. Fullbright. And this—" He looked at the man on the couch. "Who the hell is this?"

"His name is Rogers," Jon told him. "He is employed by the Royal Flush Club in Manhattan, probably as a bouncer. He came up here tonight to bring me some information and he stopped a rifle bullet fired by the man who apparently ran the first police car off the road when he was getting away. I hope no one was hurt."

"Minor injuries, but the men have been taken to the nearest hospital for a checkup. The guy showed a high beam on a curve and blinded them; they hit the ditch upside down."

"And the man got away, of course." Judy smiled sweetly at Krill.

"He got away," Krill admitted. "Who was he? You seem to know all the answers."

"Hendricks. Gordon Hendricks," Rogers told him.

"That's what Rogers thinks," Jon said.

"What do you think?"

"Somehow I don't believe that was in the cards. I'd like to check some alibis."

"You think it is one of the four you told me about over the telephone?"

"Bound to be."

"But Hendricks was one of them."

Jon nodded, unconvinced.

When Rogers had supplied the number of the Royal Flush Club, Krill telephoned, learned that Mr. Hendricks had not been there all evening. Rogers, cursing, managed with help to get to the telephone and demanded Hendricks' unlisted number, after he had identified himself. There, too, Krill drew a blank.

"Is he a hunting man?" Krill asked.

Rogers shrugged, shuffled back to the davenport. "I don't know anything about him away from the club except that he's a well-heeled broker who retired not long go and is up for an ambassadorship."

"How about asking his ex-wife?" Judy suggested.

"It has been a long time since they were married, sister," Krill reminded her.

"I know, but a man is not likely to take up a sport like hunting in his late sixties, and a woman like Mrs. Hendricks would be likely to remember and resent any interests that distracted a man's attention from her."

The lieutenant looked at her in some surprise. Because she looked so young he was not prepared to find her perceptive. Then he had the operator ring Mrs. Ellen Hendricks' number. The time was now well after midnight, but the telephone was answered almost immediately.

"Is that Mrs. Hendricks? . . . The New York police. Lieutenant Krill of Homicide . . . Yes, Homicide . . . I'm sorry to awaken you . . . Just back from the theater? Mind telling me who was in your party? . . . No, just a routine check . . . Yes, I want some information, if you can supply it . . . About your former husband . . . I understand you don't see each other now. What I want to know is whether, to your knowledge, he owns a rifle . . . I see . . . Rod and Gun Club. Uh-huh. Where? . . . Thanks very much, Mrs. Hendricks. . . . Well, not so far as we know. We'll hope he has a nice sound alibi, won't we? . . . Oh! Well, good night."

He set down the telephone. "For what it's worth, that woman would like nothing better than to see her ex-husband in trouble right up to his neck. And for your information he owns or at least he once owned a rifle, he belongs to a Rod and Gun Club somewhere in Maine, and he prided himself on getting a buck every year. Well, for the present we draw a blank on Mr. Hendricks. We don't know where he spent the evening." He smiled benevolently. "But we will."

"He was here. He shot at me," Rogers said stubbornly.

Krill looked at Jon, who said reluctantly, "It could be. But I still think Judy is the one this boy is after. He shot at a target in the light. Someone had called earlier to see whether we were here."

"Hendricks?"

"No one answered, just waited to hear my voice. And I still want more alibis."

The sergeant got to work, called Maxwell Allington, Hugh Allison *alias* Bill Bennett, and Elmer Burbank. He drew a blank except at the Burbank house, where a sleepy butler said the Burbanks were away for the weekend and he did not know where they could be reached.

"So we have a whole handful of nothing," Krill said at the end of this abortive labor. He looked at Jon and moved his head slightly, with a glance at Rogers.

"How about a drink?" Jon said, and the lieutenant agreed with alacrity. "You, Judy?"

It was his expression to which she responded. "Fine, just what I wanted."

Jon grinned and asked the lieutenant from the State Police to join them. The latter, with a glance at Krill, told his chagrined sergeant, "you can keep an eye on Rogers in case anyone is aiming for him."

In the small cardroom at the back of the house Jon served Scotch and soda to the men and plain soda to Judy.

"What's this all about, Fullbright?" Krill asked.

He told of Rogers' attempt to blackmail Hendricks and how he had come here, hoping to get money out of Jon. He expected to be fired from the Royal Flush Club and he wanted all the cash he could collect. When Jon had opened the door, someone had fired at him from near the pond. Rogers believed Hendricks had followed him to do it.

The lieutenant thought it over. "You don't believe it yourself."

"Oh, I believe Rogers. That is, he really believes what he is saying. But I don't believe Hendricks is our man."

"But you are sure he lied to you about Dolores, who was probably blackmailing him."

"Well," Judy said, "he told us he hadn't seen her in years, but he described her the way she was when I sat beside her on the subway, the dyed hair, the scars on her face, all that."

"The gal was a blackmailer," Krill said. "We had a little talk with Mrs. Collins, her former landlady—and what a joint that is! I hate to think of what we would turn up if we really went through that place. Anyhow, Mrs. Collins has had other brush-ups with the law. No record, but you can tell by the way she reacts to the police. She finally broke down and admitted she had hiked the rents ten per cent, pocketed the extra money, and hadn't told the owners. So that settles one point."

"All we need to know now," Judy said gloomily, "is what she had on Maxwell and Hugh Allison and Elmer Burbank and Gordon Hendricks. That's all. And I can just see them letting their back hair down and telling us about it. When I think I had that briefcase in my hand—"

"That's another thing," Krill said. "Speaking of the briefcase, I found the Pitten couple."

"Good work!" Jon exclaimed. "How?"

"Just routine. Got their license number and traced their car. They are in Ohio visiting a daughter whose married name is Brewster. Man out there talked to them. They don't remember the name of the moving outfit. Fact. Said it was a small operator, new business just starting, they got a flyer in the mail and thought they would try it. Bargain rates or something. We told them what we wanted and they promised, if there was a briefcase with their stuff when it arrives, they would inform us at once, but they don't plan to get to Phoenix for another ten days or two weeks."

"No!" Judy said. "I can't stand this. Anything is better than waiting, than being a target when you don't know where the shot is coming from." She could hear the hysteria in her voice, but she could not control it. "Anything is better!"

Jon took her by the shoulders and shook her. "Stop that!" As she began to cry, he said savagely, "One more peep out of you and I'll slap you silly."

She caught a long strangling breath and was still. "I guess maybe I asked for that," she said meekly, after a pause.

"I guess maybe you did. Sorry, brat, but you can't let go now. You simply can't. But if you mean that, that anything is better than waiting, we can try to smoke this guy out. That is," he looked at the lieutenant, "if we have the permission of the police department and a promise of protection."

"And what do you want to do now?" Krill demanded in some alarm.

Jon told him.

13

The story broke in the *Sentinel*. Jon had telephoned to the nearest village requesting that a copy of the paper be delivered by messenger. When it arrived, he and Judy were in the turret room looking out at a wide view of the countryside—a more heavily settled section than one would expect from driving on narrow tree-lined roads where one seemed to be alone. From this high spot one saw the houses, mostly big in this vicinity, with large grounds, winding streets, country roads, and, nearer than one would suppose, the comparatively straight broad band of a major highway.

As Jon had said, the turret was reached through a circular staircase in the wall from his bedroom to his workroom. It was an efficient rather than a decorative room, with desk, comfortable chairs, typewriter, filing cases, and card indexes.

"The story must have hit the press," Jon said.

"How do you know?"

"Look down there." He pointed to the cars beyond the pond, to the young men with press cards in their hats, to photographers setting up their equipment.

"But with a mob like that," Judy said in dismay, "our man will never take a chance on coming here."

"I didn't expect that he would come back. He is smart enough to know this place will be staked out. He'll try something else."

"What did you ask Lieutenant Krill last night—this morning—when he was leaving?"

Jon shook his head. "You know all that is good for you." He looked as fresh as though he had had a normal quota of sleep, freshly shaven, wearing a short-sleeved open shirt and lightweight slacks. He had, Judy noticed, dealt firmly with his daily woman who had been inclined to be somewhat tart when she had discovered Judy's presence. By the time he had finished a brief explanation of the situation the woman was completely subdued, appalled, and sympathetic to the girl's plight.

After less than three hours of sleep Judy was hollow-eyed, the freckles stood out on her colorless face, she started at any unexpected sound.

When Jon came running up the turret stairs and rattled the newspaper, she jumped and gave a muffled scream. "I'm sorry, Jon. I just can't help it."

He looked at her rather anxiously but decided to make light of it. "You've got a lot more guts than Rogers. There's something ridiculous about a gunman like that getting into a panic when he is shot at."

"What's happened to him?"

"I've just been on the phone to the man who guarded him last night at the hospital, though I never believed it was necessary. I still think that bullet was meant for one of us, not for Rogers. The guilty flee, and all that. Anyhow, the guard said Rogers didn't have anything but a minor wound. He didn't even need a blood transfusion, though he seemed to be bleeding a lot at first. Anyhow, he is scared as hell and begged them to let him stay there in the hospital for another day. And Krill found out from the Royal Flush Club that Rogers had got his walking papers. They didn't say why, just that he had proved to be unsatisfactory." Jon broke off to ask, "Would you like more coffee? Anything?"

Judy tried to smile. "Your cleaning woman seems to think all I need is food. You should have seen the breakfast she brought me, as though she thought it would be a kind of protection."

"She was right. Food helps." Jon added quietly, "Here it is, Judy. Brace yourself."

He turned to page three of the newspaper and spread it out on his desk. They leaned over it together. At first Judy was unexpectedly conscious of his arm brushing hers. Then she saw the story. John Milton had really gone to town on it. There was a two-column head; there were photographs of three women: the one that had already appeared of Dolores Costanza, a cabinet photograph of Margaret Morrison, and a candid camera shot of Judith Wilkins, which Peg had taken on her visit to Judy's cottage, showing her in a halter and shorts, tying up a climbing rosebush and laughing. She looked about sixteen.

Milton had done a clever job of implication. Was there any link between these women? According to Lieutenant Krill of Homicide, Judith Wilkins had assured him that she was not guilty of the murder of her roommate, Margaret Morrison, who had left her a "fortune." According to Miss Wilkins, her roommate's murder had been committed by the same man who had killed Dolores Costanza, who had died under a subway train in Times Square. Miss Costanza, said Miss Wilkins, had been attempting to blackmail four men and she had carried evidence against them in a briefcase, which she turned over to Miss Wilkins for safekeeping shortly before her murder. Lieutenant Krill had given Miss Wilkins twenty-four hours in which to produce the briefcase. She was now staying at the home of Jonathan Fullbright, the well-known writer and lecturer, who had discovered the body of Miss Morrison. There followed the address of Jon's country house.

When questioned, Lieutenant Krill had commented merely that the whole story sounded to him like a television serial. When asked whether it was true that he had given Miss Wilkins a day in which to produce the briefcase, he had merely replied, "No comment."

"Well," Judy said at last, "I asked for it."

From the foot of the stairs the cleaning woman shouted, "Telephone for you, Mr. Fullbright."

137

He called back. "I should have an extension up here," he told Judy, "but I don't like interruptions when I am working."

While he was gone, Judy reread the story. Jon had set the trap. There was nothing to do now but wait.

II

When she went downstairs, he was just putting down the telephone. "That was Krill. They had him on the carpet this morning about that story and he's even more jittery about it now than he was last night. If it pays off, he'll be all right; otherwise he'll be walking a beat. Anyhow, he has arranged for round-the-clock guards for you. But remember you are not to look for them. Just believe they are there and that you are safe. Can you do that?"

"I don't know," Judy admitted. "It's hard to have faith in protection you can't see."

"Oh, another thing; Krill got onto Hendricks. The department checked during the night and found he has a license for a hunting rifle and they've got the number of the rifle. Hendricks can't produce it; he says he lost it during a big storm last fall in Maine. He had to run for shelter and he dropped it and never found it again. He also denies absolutely shooting Rogers. He says he had tied one on and he was in his own apartment asleep and never heard the telephone. He has a houseman who goes home nights and his apartment has a self-service elevator. Not an alibi in a carload. He did break down and admit that he had Rogers fired from his job for impertinence."

The telephone rang again and Judy started. "For you," Jon said, putting the phone in her hand.

For a moment Judy stared at it as though it were a coiled snake. She tried to speak and no sound came out. Then she said, "Hello."

"Miss Wilkins? This is Gordon Hendricks."

Her wide eyes met Jon's. "Yes, Mr. Hendricks."

Jon took an involuntary step toward her and then checked himself.

"You are making a bad mistake, Miss Wilkins."

"What do you mean by that?"

"I've had the police here. Here in my apartment!" His voice shook with outrage. "I gather that you are the one who sent them to me."

"But I—"

"For your information I never even heard of the shooting of Rogers until this Lieutenant Hill, Brill, whatever the name is, came here to see me. This is intolerable and it has got to stop. I will not be persecuted."

"Well, I'm not persecuting you!" Judy said in annoyance. "Someone shot Rogers here last night and he's the one who says you did it. I didn't. As a matter of fact—"

Jon's hand shot out, caught her arm. He shook his head.

"Rogers is just sore because I had him fired for incompetence. He is getting back at me. The whole thing is a very crude maneuver. But it is extremely annoying, at a time like this."

"I should think," Judy commented, "that it would be annoying, to say the least, to be accused of attempted murder even if you weren't trying to be made ambassador."

Jon leaned back against the wall, grinning from ear to ear.

"Well, naturally—look here, Miss Wilkins, about that briefcase, I—"

"The briefcase?" As she spoke, Jon stiffened like a pointer.

"I saw that story in the *Sentinel* this morning, the one tying you in with the murder not only of your roommate but of Dolores. The story referred to four men." His voice trailed off.

Judy waited, her hand tight on the telephone.

"Did you give the police those four names?" Hendricks asked.

Again she waited.

At last he said, "I want to see you. I gathered from that story that you are in a tight spot yourself, a very tight spot; in fact, you are in danger of being arrested for murder. You seemed, if I may say so, a very attractive young lady and I should hate to think of you being involved in unpleasantness."

"Thank you, but what would you suggest, Mr. Hendricks?"

"I want to see you, to talk to you. I think I may assure you that what I have to say will be to our mutual advantage. We are in a position to help each other out of a painful situation."

"Meet you where?"

"Not there, of course. And certainly not at my apartment. I wouldn't be at all surprised if the police were watching it. Someplace quiet where we could not be overheard or overlooked."

"It sounds," Judy said, trying to speak lightly, "as though we'd have to meet in mid-Atlantic or on top of an alp."

"I am not joking," Hendricks said sharply. "This is not an amusing situation, Miss Wilkins. I should think that, in your position, you would be fully aware of its seriousness."

"I wasn't joking. I was just trying to think of a suitable place."

"Then the worst possible thing would be to attempt to find an isolated spot. Our best bet would be a crowded place. What about the cafeteria at the zoo in Central Park? We can meet there, without appearing to do so, in case one of us is followed. When you catch sight of me, you stroll away and I'll follow. When I am sure that no one is watching us, I'll talk to you."

"What time?"

"Twelve-thirty. The biggest crowd will be there at that time. And, Miss Wilkins, bring that briefcase. Understand? You won't regret it. I can guarantee that. No one has ever said I'm a stingy man. You can ask my ex-wife about that. I pay for what I want."

He hung up without waiting for a reply, and Judy repeated the conversation to Jon.

"No," he said, "I won't have it. That's too dangerous. That's just asking for it."

Judy, who had been on the brink of shrieking that she wouldn't keep the appointment, found herself changing her mind abruptly. "I'm going. You and I both know that we've got to stop this thing. I can't wait, night and day, for the sky to fall on me. I want it to be over, one way or the other."

"But you'll be terrified when the time comes."

"What do you think I am now? I'm simply petrified. But I want it over. That's all. I just want it to end. It's like having the dentist finish the job all at once instead of going back and back and dreading the next session in between times."

"All right." Unexpectedly his voice was quiet. "You'd better get into street clothes. You look better like this," and he smiled at the small figure in the halter and shorts, "but still it might attract a bit of attention in New York. And while you are changing, I'll go up and dig out a briefcase. I have several as well as an attaché case and one of those leather zippered affairs to be carried under the arm. What did the one you lost look like?"

"Brown, standard size and appearance, and quite new. Almost shiny."

"Okay. Can do."

As Judy started up the stairs, the telephone rang and Jon answered it. He looked rather queer as he turned around, his hand covering the mouthpiece. "For you again. This time it is Maxwell and he is in a tizzy."

"Judy," Maxwell exclaimed, his voice high and overwrought, "I've got to see you, angel. At once. Well, not at once, actually, because I'm right in the middle of doing a show. But say half-past three. My place. Don't say no or I'll simply crack up. I haven't had a moment's peace since I saw the story in the

141

paper. I've been blowing my lines all morning. I'm a wreck! Judy, darling, I must see you. After all, you have nothing to lose. You have Peg's money. And, after all, I mean you don't need more, do you? I simply can't raise it. But at least let me explain. It was such a little thing and I never really thought Peg cared about him all that much. Anyhow, by the way he reacted it just shows he didn't care about her. Of course I couldn't be sorrier, but I was simply in a rage and I—look, dear, please say you'll come and bring that wretched letter. I don't say I couldn't raise something; if it's strictly necessary, I might carry you until Peg's estate is settled, though I think it would be most unfair."

"Oh, for heaven's sake, stop dithering, Maxwell. You don't even wait to hear what I have to say. You keep on raising the ante. Like Bottom, you speak your whole part at once, cues and all. Just keep your head and I'll be at your place at three-thirty."

"Darling! You're wonderful. See you."

"Well," Judy said weakly when she had reported, "that's two of the four we've smoked out. But if you'll tell me how Krill's men, with the best intentions in the world, can follow me into that tiny house of Maxwell's unseen, I'd appreciate it. They'd have to be invisible men."

"Or, of course, they can get there first," Jon told her, "while Maxwell is still at the studio. And, remember, Judy, we aren't relying altogether on the police. John Milton will be around, covering his story, and so will I."

"You're coming too?"

"What the hell did you expect?"

14

Judy, in a light green sleeveless sheath the color of new leaves in spring, the stubborn curl in her hair brushed firmly into a wave, high heels on small feet, seemed older and more sophisticated than Jon had ever seen her. At the same time she seemed intolerably vulnerable. She was so small, so defenseless.

"Where on earth are we going?" she asked in surprise.

He had rolled the Plymouth out of the garage, pushed it around onto a narrow dirt path through the woods behind the house, which was little more than a track. "It's a bit longer this way and it will bring us out onto the main road a couple of miles farther north, but we have to lose those boys in front of the house somehow or other."

"But what about the police guard? Won't we lose them too?"

"I called Krill to report developments and inform him of our movements. I asked him to notify the State Police, so we should be covered from this end until we reach Manhattan. I also asked my daily woman to stay on and take telephone messages. I told her clearly what your plans are and where you will be, so you can easily be traced if anyone wants to do so. We still have two more candidates to hear from, you know."

They exchanged few words on the way into New York. Because of the heavy storm of the afternoon before, the temperature had dropped to endurable limits, a little over eighty, with a light breeze and low humidity. Even when the city canyons closed in on them, there was no great discomfort.

"Aren't you going to leave the car at your garage?" Judy asked in surprise when he passed the place, going east on Ninety-sixth Street.

"Whoever followed us to and from Danbury knows this is my regular garage. I'll park under the Coliseum and we'll get taxis there."

When they came up from the basement garage, Jon looked carefully around before he hailed a taxi and put Judy in it. "Just keep your head." His hand closed over hers. "Don't panic. Remember you are not alone. You've got a regular army of protectors all around you." He gave her his brown briefcase. "All right?"

She smiled at him. "All right." She tried to sound confident.

Fortunately she had a preoccupied driver and not a talkative one. She sat looking over her shoulder. With a little sigh of relief she saw Jon climb into a taxi that pulled into traffic behind her own. Everything was going to be all right.

When she had paid the driver, she walked swiftly toward the cafeteria, careful to keep her eyes straight ahead, although the temptation to look behind her was almost more than she could withstand.

She did not bother with a tray, got iced coffee, and strolled around casually holding it, sipping now and then. She had a legitimate excuse now for looking at tables, as though seeking for an empty place to sit down. At one she saw a tall shabby fellow in a wrinkled seersucker suit. John Milton was eating a cheese sandwich and drinking iced tea. He met her eyes and looked back at the table, reaching for sugar. She went on without another glance at him but with a lift of the heart. I'm not alone, she told herself. I'm not alone. It's going to be all right.

She almost failed to recognize Gordon Hendricks, who was coatless, had removed his necktie, and rolled up his shirt sleeves. He wore dark glasses. When he caught sight of her, he was lighting a cigarette and he held his lighter motionless, his eyes on the brown briefcase that swung from her hand. For the first time Judy found something amusing in the situation. Hendricks had done all he could to submerge the would-be ambassador and the former broker in the coatless and tieless man at the cafeteria table, but he had forgotten to replace his gold cigarette lighter with a strip of matches.

She went past his table, walked on, stopped for a few minutes to watch the sea lions, wondering how they could endure this placid spot after the fury of the surf that was their natural element. Did sea lions have attacks of nerves or suffer from frustrations? The thought occupied her while she strolled along a path, away from the zoo, away from the crowd. She was surprised to discover how calm she felt. Perhaps it was only in the dark that fears engulfed her. Here in the sunlight, in this green oasis, everything seemed all right. Nevertheless there was a twitching between her shoulder blades which she could not control, as though she were wincing away from a rifle bullet. She felt horribly exposed.

She walked slowly. An uninhibited young couple lay in each other's arms on the grass. Either they did not care about privacy or they lived under conditions that never provided any, for they seemed oblivious of the passing strollers. A man on a bench was feeding squirrels from a paper bag of peanuts. A couple of young mothers with babies in strollers chatted on a nearby bench. There was a man engrossed in a crossword puzzle. He looked at Judy, looked at the briefcase, and began to fold his paper. Under his loose-fitting jacket Judy was prepared to swear there was a shoulder holster. That must be Krill's man.

"This will do," Hendricks said from behind her in the mellifluous voice that seemed out of place with his present style of dress.

Judy, who had not heard his approach, turned with a nervous start. He indicated a bench that provided a clear view around them. No one could approach without being seen. She sat down beside him but put the briefcase on the far side, fingers gripping the handle.

Hendricks took off his dark glasses and she saw that his eyes were puffy and reddened. He had prepared himself with a bag of peanuts. As an inquisitive and hopeful squirrel approached them, he tossed out a peanut.

"Though I must say," he commented, "it looks as though it were well nourished."

"There are rats in the park, too," Judy said in her clear voice. "Not such nice company."

"Let's get down to business. I don't want to be seen with you, not after that story in the *Sentinel*. Let's get this over in a hurry. But first, what really happened last night? What's the true story about Rogers?"

"He came up to Mr. Fullbright's house to give him some information about you and Miss Costanza. Before he could speak, he was shot from across the pond by a rifle. The man got away. Rogers said you were the one who did it and, so far as we know, you are the only one who owns a rifle, and certainly the only one with any motive for killing Rogers."

"I had no motive whatsoever for killing Rogers. He was as harmless to me as a six-months baby. No threat at all. He tried bluffing and found out what it got him. A lost job. And that took care of that."

John Milton was strolling along a distant path. He stopped to take a quick picture of some small boys shooting marbles. He did not look in their direction.

"But you had lied to us about Dolores Costanza. You lied when you said you had not seen her in years. The way you described her was the way she looked when she died, not when you were supposed to have known her. And she threatened you. Rogers told us so."

"I didn't kill her, Miss Wilkins. In my own way I'm a gambler, but I know when the odds are too great. And Dolores wasn't worth it. God knows she got plenty out of me when she finally realized I had no intention of marrying her. Anything for a quiet life. It's true she could have lost me that appointment. What a fool I was to give her free run of my apartment when we were together! I should have known she would go poking and prying. But even if she had given the story to the press, as she threatened, I still have plenty to live for. I'm a rich man and I like living. I don't intend to jeopardize what I have. But I want that briefcase. I am willing to pay you twenty-five thousand dollars. We'll go to my bank now and you'll have the money in your hand before you surrender it. Fair enough?"

Judy stood up. She had not been prepared for instant action. She was not sure what she was supposed to do next.

"Wait. First I've got to see what I am buying. I'm not shelling out a penny for a pig in a poke. Sit down and open that briefcase."

Judy hesitated. With a sudden movement Hendricks wrenched the leather case out of her hand. He bent over, his face intent as he unstrapped it. There was a click and he looked up, startled, to see John Milton taking his picture. He turned on Judy, and there was no trace of the ambassador now. There was stark fury in his face. "You dirty, double-crossing little—"

The man who had been doing the crossword puzzle was suddenly beside them, reaching for the briefcase.

Hendricks looked from face to face. Then he got to his feet and broke into a shambling run, heading for the exit onto Fifth Avenue.

II

"Well!" Judy sank back on the bench.

The detective put the briefcase in her hand. "You all right, miss?"

"Yes, thanks. Are you just going to let him go?"

"Are you prepared to swear out a complaint against him?"

"Oh, no!"

Milton came up, grinning. "That was a nice picture. Very nice. What happened? All at once the action seemed to be getting serious."

"He offered me twenty-five thousand dollars for the briefcase. He said we could go to his bank right away for the money, but he wanted to see first what he was buying. And he denied shooting Rogers or killing Dolores. He said Rogers couldn't injure him and that, though Dolores could have lost him his appointment, he had a lot to live for and he didn't gamble against odds."

"Did he tell you what she had on him?"

Judy shook her head. "Apparently she snooped around his apartment in the days when she was still hoping he would marry her and stole some papers, which must be important."

"But why hold them so long? How much time has passed? Ten to fifteen years, isn't it?"

"I don't know. Perhaps she didn't understand what they meant, perhaps she wasn't desperate for money, perhaps they wouldn't have done him any harm until he wanted a diplomatic career."

The strangest element of the whole situation to Judy was that the incident had attracted no attention. Older people continued to chat on nearby benches, younger people lay on the grass absorbed in each other, children played and shouted. A determined and joyless jogger went past, knees moving like pistons. A man strolled along, absorbed in his thoughts, walking for his health. Compared with the bronzed jogger, his face was pale as though from a long illness.

"What are you staring at?" Jon demanded, coming up unexpectedly.

"The handsomest man I ever saw in my life."

"You'd better keep your mind on the job you have to do," he said so irritably that she was taken aback.

Milton looked from one revealing face to the other and then grinned in enlightenment.

The detective said, "I'll drift off for now. But I'll be around."

"What about Maxwell's little house?" she asked.

"We'll have it staked before he quits work. There is a guy at the television studio now, keeping an eye on him. But the lieutenant thinks we can wash him out. He hasn't found Allington's alibi, the man he was supposed to see off at La Guardia at the time when some-one was trying to smother you. But he did better than that. He found a cop at the airfield whose wife is a fan of this actor's, and he asked Allington for an autograph. Remembers the incident well. So unless there is more than one person involved in this mess, Allington seems to be in the clear."

"What happens now?" Milton asked.

Jon answered, "Judy and I will lunch at the Algon-quin. You buzz off or you'll have every reporter in town on our trail."

Milton nodded amiably and sauntered away.

"So far it's a washout, isn't it?" Judy asked.

"What I can't understand," Jon admitted, "is a man like Hendricks panicking and running away. What the hell does he think is in that briefcase? I'd have ex-pected him to bluff out the situation."

"So far nothing has worked the way we expected, has it?"

"You aren't losing your nerve, are you?"

"I don't think so, but all the time I was walking along the path I expected to get a bullet in the back. I've had nicer feelings."

"Shall we call this off? It's still not too late."

"But we are committed now."

"Krill can issue a statement calling the whole news story a hoax. It will clear him with the department anyhow."

"And sell Milton straight down the river."

"Well, something has to give."

Judy struggled for a moment with an overwhelm-ing temptation to say yes. Then she shook her head decisively. "We'll do it the way we planned it. If I

149

don't stick this out, I'll go on being afraid of that bullet in the back."

At the Fifth Avenue entrance to the park Jon looked around and waited until there was only one taxi in sight before he signaled to it.

"The Algonquin." He spent most of the trip looking over his shoulder, but when Judy said inquiringly, "Sister Anne?" he shook his head.

In the lobby of the Algonquin he encountered his literary agent, who was accompanied by a well-known novelist. They were celebrating pre-publication sale of a new novel to the movies. The agent welcomed Jon and suggested that they join forces for lunch. After a look at Judy, the novelist seconded the suggestion enthusiastically.

Having offered a toast to the new book, the agent turned to Jon. "What have you been getting yourself involved in? First, that girl who was to do research for you at *New Trends,* Margaret Morrison, was murdered and you found her body. The police called me, wanting to know all about you. You know what they say: The one who claims to find the body is usually the criminal. Now Miss Morrison's roommate and heir is up to her ears in murder, and living, and I quote, under your protection. What—"

Belatedly the agent saw Jon's face and Judy's expression. He broke off in dismay. "Look here, I'm always running off at my big mouth. I'm terribly sorry."

Momentarily Jon was too angry to speak.

"People are bound to gossip about us, I suppose," Judy said. "I just hadn't thought about that part of it. I was too scared."

Seeing her distress and embarrassment, Jon smiled at her. "Considering that her roommate was murdered, that one attempt has been made to smother her and another to shoot her, Judy has had a rather trying few days. There's been no time to worry about gossip, as she says. In any case—"

"No, Jon!" Judy broke in. "You needn't think you have to make an honest woman of me because of all this. Mid-Victorian heroics are out of character for you."

"Anyhow," the novelist declared, "Fullbright is the wrong type for you. Benedick the bachelor. Wouldn't do at all. He'd bore you to death in a week. Why don't you have dinner with me tomorrow evening and let us explore this matter further?"

"That's an idea," Judy admitted. "Provided, of course, I'm still alive."

15

The brown briefcase was swinging in her hand as she walked into the lobby of the big apartment building in the Village. The detective from Central Park was seated in a big chair, again working on a crossword puzzle. He glanced at her and away without a sign of recognition. Judy passed him, went out a door at the far end, and crossed the small sunbaked strip of ground to Maxwell's tiny house.

He must have been on the lookout, because he flung open the door before she reached it. "Angel! I've simply been on the rack, thinking you wouldn't come."

He put her fussily into his most comfortable chair, adjusted the electric fan so that the breeze would be directly on her.

"A drink?"

She shook her head.

He curled up on the rug at her feet and she recalled that he had taken the same position in *Pot of Gold*. It was boyishly engaging in a way but, unfortunately, from this position she could see a small round bald spot on his head, which spoiled the illusion.

"I suppose," he confided, "you think I'm a perfect monster. But I will say this in my own defense. I never believed Peg was really in love with the man. You know that manner of hers, so detached. She certainly did not emanate any aura of youthful infatuation or anything of that kind. As a matter of fact, she treated him as though he were her property, something to parade around. You know the sort of thing: she had fulfilled her woman's mission of getting a man."

"Look here," Judy said furiously, "you are talking about Peg. Remember? Your cousin. My best friend. And she has been murdered, her skull cr—" She got hold of herself with an effort.

Maxwell seemed deeply offended by her attitude. "I'm sorry," he said stiffly. "I was just trying to explain. I agree that Peg had all the virtues, and I think her death was simply monstrous, but just the same, darling, she could be cold and unfeeling. It's only fair to see my side of it."

"All right, let's see your side of it."

Maxwell was silent for so long that she looked down at him in surprise. He seemed to be absorbed in tracing the pattern in the rug with a forefinger.

"The show I was in got a low rating and it was taken off. During the summer, too, when there isn't much doing. I even had to make a couple of commercials. That's when I came across Dolores Costanza. Stopped to chat, wondering if she had heard of any openings, new shows, something like that—you'd be surprised how many people land jobs through word-of-mouth tips—and we had a drink together."

Again he became absorbed with the pattern in the rug. He did not look up. "Well, I'd bought this little place; tiny, of course, but different. It's so important to be different. Anyhow, what with one thing and another, and I'd had to have three new suits made to order, I was a bit short of cash and I couldn't meet the mortgage payments. So I asked Peg. She said she never lent money to anyone. She quoted Polonius, that old bore, to me. And she said if I was short I'd be wise to go back to the bank and talk about new financing for the house. Well, really!"

He got up to look for cigarettes and, after offering them to Judy, which she refused, he lighted one and returned to his position at her feet.

"I'll probably die of cancer, but I'm just so overwrought I have to do something. Anyhow, while I was at Peg's talking about a small loan, her fiancé came in. Did you ever meet him?"

Judy shook her head. "I sort of gathered there had been an engagement, but she never mentioned the man. Something must have made her a bit disillusioned about people in general."

Maxwell looked up sharply, looked down again. "He was a big guy. Name of Meadows. Lewis Meadows. He had just dropped by for something and we left Peg's together. I was sore. Well, naturally. Peg with all that money and earning a darned good salary besides and not willing to part with a cent. Well, I mean! So he suggested that we stop for a quick one. He knew I was upset, and I suppose he was curious; he didn't know much about Peg's family and background and general financial situation, and I could see he was simply panting to find out.

"I told him Peg had refused to make a small loan, though I didn't want much and she knew I'd pay it back as soon as I was working again. And then—you know how you get carried away. I mean I was really furious with Peg. He was defending her, trying to draw me out. Well," his forefinger dug at the pattern as though trying to uproot it, "when I got home I was still smoldering. An artist's temperament, you know."

Oh, not that, Judy protested to herself.

"So I wrote him a little note, saying I was sorry I had said such bitchy things about Peg. Quite unjustified, because I knew she had lost her money and simply did not have it to lend. And, well, he drifted away and more or less forced her, out of sheer pride, into breaking the engagement. How she found out—I mean, when it was too late and they had broken up, he discovered she was really in the chips. I suppose he tried to patch things up with her but it didn't work. Then he wrote me a letter, saying what he thought of me. He practically threatened that he would knock me sidewise if he ever caught sight of me, and he said he'd like to know how long I would keep my job and manage to go on looking like a cut-rate Sir Galahad if the public knew the truth about me. Things like that. Too shattering!"

Maxwell looked dubiously at Judy to measure her reaction to the story, half hoping to find her sympathetic.

"Anyhow," he went on, "like a fool I kept the letter in a drawer in my dressing room. I thought if he ever did attack me, I'd have proof as to who did it. Well, as it happened, Dolores dropped in one day for a drink and a chat—this was after I was working regularly, and probably *forever,* my dear, in *Pot of Gold.* Poor dear Dolores was looking for a tip about jobs doing commercials. At the time I was working on the set and she went through the drawer and took the letter. I never knew it until she called me up and said she wanted five thousand dollars for it or the story would leak out to a gossip columnist who was willing to run the risk of a libel suit."

Maxwell crushed his cigarette with shaking fingers and immediately took another out of the package. "I didn't kill Dolores. I didn't kill Peg. I swear to God I didn't. I am not a violent man, Judy. You believe that, don't you? Tell me that you believe it."

She nodded, realized that he could not see her while his head was bowed down and that absurd bald spot so in evidence. "Oh, yes, I believe that. You're not violent, Maxwell; you are just vindictive and unscrupulous and untrustworthy. No wonder Peg lost faith in people. She had a rotten deal, didn't she?"

He wriggled uncomfortably, got up to take a small can of tomato juice from the refrigerator, open it, and pour it over ice. He added vodka. He drank slowly while Judy waited. At last he said, "Well, you know all about it now. If you want to avenge Peg and get even with me, you can tell people the whole thing and that will just about put the lid on my career."

"But it wouldn't help the situation, would it?"

The actor brightened. "Of course not! Then you won't—that is, will you give me back that letter?"

Judy took a long breath. Then she made up her mind. "I don't have the letter, Maxwell."

The boyish face wasn't boyish at all as he looked at her. She put out a hand to ward him off, at something she saw in that distorted face. "Wait! That is really true." She told him how she had disposed of the briefcase with its incriminating material. She opened the one Jon had given her to prove to him that it was empty.

"Then why," he demanded, "did you come here? What are you trying to accomplish? What was that story in the *Sentinel?* Those four men who were blackmailed by Dolores, that twenty-four-hour notice the police have given you. Was all that a trick?"

"There are four men and one of them has tried twice to kill me. But I know now, at least I feel fairly sure, that it wasn't you, Maxwell. But you can see that I had to eliminate the possibility."

"Eliminate me!" His voice was shrill with rage and fear. "By coming here you may have involved me in all kinds of danger. I think this is a frightful thing for you to do. Getting me mixed up in your problems. I want you to go away right now. You understand? Right now!" He was livid with panic.

"Oh, don't be so stupid! No one is going to hurt you." Judy got up, restrapped the briefcase, and went to the door. Maxwell stood watching her. She crossed the hot little strip of bare ground and entered the big lobby. The detective was not in sight. Around the corner someone was speaking over a telephone. The only person in evidence was the very pale man whom she had seen earlier in Central Park. She wondered now whether he was a replacement for the other detective; otherwise it was too much of a coincidence for him to reappear in this way.

She went past him toward the street, hoping that Jon would be waiting for her somewhere nearby. She had a moment's awareness that someone was near her and then her head seemed to explode.

II

There were a number of heads behaving in an erratic manner, whirling around in space so that Judy had to close her eyes to shut them out.

"She's all right, I tell you," a voice said firmly. "Just knocked out. No damage at all. She'll have a headache for a while. Nothing more."

"We ought to get her to a hospital." Jon sounded worried. "See she has X-rays."

"Nonsense," the first man said.

Judy risked opening her eyes once more, and this time she found the heads stationary and attached to bodies in the customary way. The authoritative voice appeared to belong to a doctor who was holding a black bag and preparing to leave.

Jon knelt beside her, his expression grim. Beyond him stood the reporter, Milton, and the detective who, this time, was not bothering with crossword puzzles. After looking from face to face, Judy began to chuckle, though her head throbbed when she moved it. She was sitting in a big chair in the lobby of the apartment building and the detective was telling curious spectators to move on.

"That trap went off with a great big bang," Judy announced.

"Krill loves this," the detective said. "I just called in. They'll probably make him turn in his badge. They'll collect mine, too. I was watching Allington's house and listening to that talk you had with him. What a guy! I ducked out of sight around the side of the house when you left. By the time I reached the lobby you had had it. Out like a light."

"I'm to blame," Jon said. "This was my bright idea."

"I suppose he got the briefcase." In spite of the lancing pain through her head, Judy laughed. "I wish I could have seen his face when he opened it."

"I wish I could see his face. Period." Jon was bitter.

157

"So we lose our last chance at the guy," Milton commented. "Well, I can draw unemployment insurance. For a while at least."

"I don't see why you are all so darned down in the mouth," Judy said. "If I can take it, why can't you? And I'm not even going to make any dirty cracks about the kind of bodyguards you turned out to be. So let's forget this and get on with the job."

"How?" Milton asked.

"Well, we could go ask him for the briefcase in a polite sort of way and see how he reacts."

The detective did a double take. "You mean you saw the guy? You know who he is?"

"I thought at first he was one of your men. I saw him hanging around in Central Park when Hendricks was talking to me. Then he turned up in the lobby here as I was coming across from Maxwell's house. He didn't speak to me, just for a second I felt someone behind me, and there was no one else, so—"

"Could you describe him?"

"It was the beautiful one. The handsome man with the pale face as though—oh!"

"Where does it hurt?" Jon demanded.

"I don't hurt. I was just remembering. Miss Goody." Jon looked blank.

"Mr. Burbank's secretary," she said impatiently. "Don't you remember? She told us about Dolores saying Bill Bennett was hiding his beautiful face behind all that hair. But suppose he shaved it off. There's no other man involved in this business who is spectacularly handsome. And we always knew Bennett or Allison or whoever he is had the best reason for killing Dolores: those years in prison and her threat of revealing his identity to Mr. Burbank. Like all the rest of them, he is terrified of that sensitive industry."

Rather unsteadily, Judy managed to get to her feet. "What are we waiting for? If we give him too much time, he will get rid of the briefcase and there will go our proof."

"You aren't going anywhere," Jon told her. "This is the third attempt on you."

"What do you suggest I do to be safe, unless you have me arrested?"

"By God, I'd like to put you in protective custody until this thing is over."

"And since you can't do that, let's get moving. Come on, for heaven's sake!"

They piled into a taxi and Jon gave the address of Bill Bennett's apartment on Riverside Drive. Judy was wedged between him and Milton, with the detective on the jump seat.

As they started into the building, she commented, "We will look like a delegation."

"It doesn't matter what we look like." Jon had taken her arm and held it so tightly that he hurt her. "You stay back. Is that clear?"

"Yes, suh, Massa Fullbright. Yes, indeedy."

The young man at the switchboard looked up at them, frowning, because, for a moment, they were silhouetted against the light. Then he recognized Jon. "Mr. Fullbright! I was just getting it down on paper." As Jon looked blank, he explained, "About your book."

"Oh, fine. Is Mr. Bennett in?"

"I haven't seen him." He plugged in and rang several times, then looked up to shake his head.

"Will you admit us to his apartment?"

"Sorry, but we aren't permitted to do that."

The detective showed his badge.

"Mr. Bennett isn't in trouble, is he?"

"I'll get a search warrant, if you like," the detective told him.

"What has he done? Why do you want him?"

"Murder."

After a moment of hesitation the young man took them up in the elevator, knocked at a door, knocked repeatedly, looked at the detective and, at his gesture, took out a key.

The detective put a restraining hand on the young

man's arm as he started to open the door. "I'll go first." He eased his gun out of its shoulder holster and went inside, gesturing for the others to remain where they were. Jon pushed Judy behind him. There was a long pause. The detective had taken a few steps and then he had stopped abruptly. They heard him dial a number and speak in a low tone.

Then he was standing in the open doorway. "Just look but don't touch anything. Who is he?"

The man from the switchboard stared at the man who sat at a desk, his head bowed on his hands. He bent down to peer into his face. Then he straightened up slowly, shaking his head. "I never saw him before. Is he dead?"

"Very," the detective said.

"Who killed him? Not Mr. Bennett."

Judy had pushed past Jon, bent over to take a look at the man's face. She reached out her hand and found Jon's waiting for it, warm and comforting. "That's the beautiful one. I think he must be Hugh Allison."

"*Alias* Bill Bennett," Milton said in a tone of relief. He pointed to the open and empty briefcase on the desk. "So that wraps up the case. Not murder. Suicide. I suppose that was the only way the poor devil had left." He turned to the detective. "May I use that telephone?"

"Wait," Jon told him. "Don't go out on a limb."

"What's that supposed to mean?"

"If I'm not all wrong," Jon said, "this isn't suicide. It's another murder."

16

"So!" Lieutenant Krill said sadly. "Dr. Livingstone, I presume."

"I suppose," Jon conceded, "this is all very funny to you."

Krill ignored his tone. He looked at Judy. "You keep turning up, don't you? You are supposed to be recuperating from that mugging you got in the lobby of a Greenwich Village apartment. And before that, I understand, you had an interesting interview in Central Park."

"Doing your work for you," Judy reminded him.

"And who is this?" The lieutenant stared down at the dead man at the desk.

"That is the man who knocked me out in the Village and stole the briefcase." Judy gestured toward the discarded, empty case. "I think his name is Hugh Allison but that he has been living under the name of Bill Bennett since he got out of prison."

"And why do you think that?" Krill was jovial.

"Because Allison was described by two women as beautiful, and Bennett had a big beard, and this man is so—so pale, as though his skin had been covered, and I wondered if he had just shaved off his beard."

At Krill's gesture the switchboard operator withdrew in relief, after agreeing not to say anything about what had happened.

"All right." Krill gestured for them all to withdraw to the hallway and make room for his own squad— fingerprint men, photographers, doctor, a disciplined group that worked rapidly and efficiently.

161

"So," the lieutenant said when they were down in the lobby, "I take it that Allison, or Bennett, saw Milton's story in the *Sentinel,* checked to find out where you were, trailed you to the Village to steal the briefcase, and then took poison when he found the case was empty."

"I doubt it," Jon said. "I believe he was murdered."

"You certainly want everything the hard way."

"I don't want any part in all this," Jon assured him.

"First," Krill decided, "we've got to establish the guy's identity. If he is Allison, we'll turn up his fingerprints."

"First," Jon told him, "we do something to protect Judy. Up to now we haven't done so well."

"But the guy is dead."

"Allison, or Bennett, is dead."

"Then who the hell—"

"I don't know. But every time we take our eyes off this girl, she is in trouble: nearly smothered, nearly shot, nearly killed by a blow over the head. How many more of these things is she supposed to take?"

"There's no doubt, is there, that this man upstairs is the one who hit her over the head?" Krill said.

"He must have been," Judy told him. "There was no one else in the lobby, and he got the briefcase."

"Then Fullbright thinks two men are going around slugging women, is that it?"

"I want the girl safe," Jon replied stubbornly.

Krill gave an exaggerated sigh and turned to the detective. "Take them down to Headquarters and keep them until I get there."

"Charge them?"

"Good God, no! Just keep this girl out of trouble, if you can. Now get going. I have things to do and I don't need her help in doing them."

"I found Allison for you," Judy pointed out.

"You found him dead for me," he corrected.

The afternoon passed slowly. A police station is not designed for comfort. While Milton chatted with the sergeant at the desk, Judy sat wearily beside Jon, not attempting to talk.

Finally she asked, "Jon, was the lieutenant right? Was I responsible for the death of that poor man?"

"He was murdered because he went looking for that briefcase," Jon said, and a man waiting disconsolately on a bench near them turned to give them a startled look and move farther off.

"It couldn't have been Maxwell. He was still in his house when we got into the taxi."

"So we're left with Burbank and Hendricks."

"Somehow, after the way Hendricks scuttled off in Central Park, I don't believe he would make another try for that briefcase."

"So then we have Elmer Burbank."

"But why, Jon, why? There's no reason to believe that poor devil didn't poison himself."

It was late afternoon when Krill came in, waved them to his own small office, took off his jacket with relief, loosened his necktie, and sank back in his chair. He was tired and hot, but he managed to grin at Judy. "You've stayed out of trouble all this time?" he exclaimed in pleased surprise.

Jon started to speak, but Krill waved his hand for silence and began to look over the reports on his desk. At length he leaned back in his chair and lighted a cigarette.

"Well, we've got identification. The fingerprints of the dead man are those of Hugh Allison. They match up with the ones all over the apartment, so he was also Bill Bennett. We got hold of Mrs. Hendricks, who brought along a rather dim picture of Allison. Anyhow, she recognized him at once. And we got Miss Goody up there, Burbank's secretary. She—it's a funny thing, because she seems businesslike and not at all sentimental. She looked and looked and said what a pity that such a handsome man had concealed his fine looks all those years. And, by the way, that beard of his was shaved off within the last day or so and he'd tried to scrape up all the hair into a paper bag that was in the wastebasket."

"How far does that take us?"

"Allison swallowed a cyanide pill. Works fast. Miss Goody says he would never have killed himself and left an unfinished story. It was one he was quite excited about. She is convinced that he was murdered."

"So am I," Jon told him.

"It narrows down," Judy said in a small voice; "Maxwell is out; Allison is dead."

"And Hendricks," Krill pushed aside papers, selected a report, "left for Washington on the two o'clock train."

"Leaving Burbank," Jon said. "I suppose you haven't got hold of him yet."

"The Burbanks and their children have a cottage somewhere at Montauk. He's out fishing. We talked to Mrs. Burbank by telephone. She'll have him call us as soon as he gets in."

"Leaving no one at all," Judy said.

A policeman came in with a report which he put before the lieutenant. The latter glanced at it, drew it toward him, read slowly.

"At the risk of making a nuisance of myself," Jon said, "what I want to know is what do we do to keep Judy safe until this thing is wrapped up?"

Krill looked at him, looked back at the report. For a moment he meditated, blowing smoke rings. Then he pushed the report across the desk to Jon.

"Sometimes," he said, "the police, in their stodgy way, get results. Especially when they aren't handicapped by any brilliant side play from the amateurs."

"What he means by this," Jon explained to Judy, "is that the police have discovered the moving concern that handled the Pitten lares and penates; they have found the van in Indianapolis, and a briefcase was hidden under a pile of sacking."

"Oh." Judy exclaimed, "that's what it was. I can remember now that rough texture."

"As we seem to have no alternative but protective

164

custody," the lieutenant suggested to Jon, "how would you like to take the young lady to Indianapolis to collect the briefcase? That would keep her out of harm's way for another few hours." He added dubiously, "Maybe."

Jon stretched out his arm. "May I telephone to make reservations for plane seats?"

"We'll handle that. You keep an eye on the girl and bring her back alive."

II

"I haven't even a toothbrush," Judy said rather breathlessly when she found herself in a police car headed for the airport.

"Even in Indian territory beyond the Hudson," Jon explained gravely, "there are toothbrushes to be had."

When the great city had fallen behind and they had unbuckled their seat belts, they sipped martinis. They ate dinner almost without exchanging a word, each sunk in his own thoughts.

It was Judy who said at last, "In the beginning I didn't know where to hide. Now I don't see much reason for it. Because there is no one left. Every suspect has been eliminated."

"But three people have been eliminated by murder. That wasn't the work of a nonexistent person."

"Then we have to start all over, don't we?"

"We'll end, where we started, with the briefcase."

"What do you think we'll find in it?"

"We? Krill would take a dim view of our opening that briefcase on our own. We turn it over to him."

"And that's all?" she asked blankly. "Then we might never know. Jon, I don't think I could bear that. I can't spend the rest of my life running away."

Jon did not speak for a long time. When he did, he took her aback. "How did you like Owens?"

"Owens?"

"The novelist we met at lunch."

"Oh."

"Well," Jon's voice was edged with irritation, "what do you intend to do?"

"About what?"

"About Owens. He said I wasn't your type. Remember? He told you that you'd better have dinner with him tomorrow so you could explore the situation."

"Oh."

When she did not go on, Jon said, "For a girl who can talk too much you don't seem to have much to say now." He sounded very ill-tempered indeed.

Judy smiled at him. "After all," she said demurely, "a girl has to look after herself. Owens certainly seems to be available. And it makes a nice change."

"From what?" Jon was scowling.

"Benedick the bachelor. The man who lives alone and likes it. The man who puts up such a valiant fight for his freedom and independence."

"I've never been the small-minded kind of man who feels he has to be consistent. And, if you remember Benedick, he married the girl and liked it." He found her hand, which was lying conveniently near his, and held it tightly. He cleared his throat. "Judy—"

A sign flashed on and he released her hand to fasten his seat belt, to check hers.

It was still light when they walked down the ramp at Indianapolis, Jon holding Judy's arm. "We're going to be chaperoned," he told her.

The man was not in uniform, but he might as well have been. His weight, carriage, and expression all proclaimed police as clearly as though he had worn a placard. He eyed the descending passengers and came without hesitation to Jon.

"Mr. Fullbright?" He showed his badge. "New York asked me to give you any help I could. I'm Carruthers."

"Thank you. This is Miss Wilkins."

Judy shook hands, smiling. "How did you know which ones we were?"

"Lieutenant Krill described you over the telephone." Carruthers grinned reminiscently.

"What did he say?" Judy demanded.

"That you are small and blond, with eyes as big as saucers but that don't miss a trick. Whistle-bait, he called you."

Judy laughed. She was in an uncertain mood. Jon's interrupted speech had made her feel as though she were breathing champagne bubbles. "Where do we go now?"

"We're going back to New York on the next plane. We have the briefcase." She noticed then the brown briefcase in his hand. "Is this the one all the fuss was about?"

She looked at it. "Well, they are all more or less alike, aren't they?" She lifted it. "It feels heavy like the one I put in the moving van and it has the same kind of tiny padlock."

To her disappointment the detective took it back. "That's our plane." He led the way across the field.

"You're going with us?" Jon asked.

The detective met his eyes over Judy's head. "Krill thinks this thing is dynamite. Said three people had been murdered to get possession of it, and the young lady had had some trouble. So it seemed better for me to come along and take it back."

"Then there was really no point in our coming out here at all, was there?" Judy asked.

"So far as I can make out, the lieutenant was trying to keep you under wraps for a few hours."

While the detective had a drink and ate dinner, they sipped highballs and waited for the lights of New York. Judy's eyes kept straying to the briefcase.

"What's in it?" she asked. "What in heaven's name is in it that matters so much?"

The detective shook his head. "We haven't tried to open it. This is strictly New York's baby. We have enough trouble without saddling ourselves with a three-time killer."

"But you've had to go to all this trouble just to protect me!" Judy exclaimed.

Carruthers smiled. "No man in his right mind would kick about that." He whistled softly. "Anyhow," he added rather hastily, as he saw Jon's expression, "it isn't safe to ship dynamite without the proper precautions." He stared out of the window, looking down on the incredible beauty of New York after dark. "And there are other compensations. I don't get many opportunities to see the big city. God! What a sight."

As the light flashed on, he buckled his belt and reached for the brown briefcase, which had never been more than a few inches from his hand.

17

There was some delay while Krill was summoned from his apartment on West End Avenue. By the time he reached his office, Milton was pacing up and down the room, chain-smoking, the detective from Indianapolis was exchanging trade gossip with the desk sergeant, and Jon and Judy waited, their eyes fixed on the brown briefcase as though it were a rattlesnake coiled to strike.

Krill took a quick look around as he came in and then he too looked at the brown briefcase. "You've identified it?"

Judy shrugged helplessly. "Well, it looks the same and it's about the same weight."

"Did it have that padlock?"

She nodded.

At Krill's orders a man came in, tinkered for a moment, and opened the padlock. Everyone in the room took an involuntary step forward as the lieutenant removed the padlock and unstrapped the briefcase. He cleared his desk with a swift impatient gesture and then emptied the contents of the briefcase on it.

While he started sorting out and examining papers, Judy clenched and unclenched her hands, her eyes never leaving that mass of papers on the desk.

Krill looked up, eyebrows raised. "Quite a nice guy, our friend Maxwell Allington," he said. "This is the letter he was in such a dither about." He pushed it across the table to Jon, who read it and handed it on to Judy, who repeated the process with Milton.

"Only," she told the reporter, "it isn't fair to make use of that. Poor Maxwell is scared enough. And it's the past."

"I can't use it, anyhow," Milton said. "My editor does not like libel suits. And, hell, Maxwell isn't the kind of news he thinks he is. Somehow I doubt that many of the people who watch his program can even read."

Jon laughed. "There's that, of course."

"But," Milton reminded him, "I am not following you around for my health. I expect a story."

"You'll get one."

At Jon's confident tone Judy looked at him but there was, as usual, nothing to read in his face.

The bulkiest mass of material in the briefcase was stapled together between blue cardboard covers. Krill tried to skim it, then went back and attempted to read it more slowly. He shook his head. "This would take a financial expert. I'll get someone on it tomorrow."

"I covered the financial news at the *Sentinel* for three long years," Milton said, and Krill pushed the big package across the desk to him.

While Milton began to cast an expert eye over the material, Krill picked up a number of newspaper clippings that had been fastened together. He spread them out and discovered that they reported the arrest, trial, and conviction of Hugh Allison, bank teller, who had robbed his bank of more than $30,000 and had been unable to make restitution. The story had not been an unusual one and Allison had been only a minor clerk, so not much space was devoted to it. There was, however, a picture of the Allison of fifteen years ago, slimmer, gayer, a singularly handsome man who believed in his world, himself, and his future.

Clipped to it was a letter, dated ten days earlier, addressed to Dolores Costanza at the hotel in the West Forties.

"Before I let you ruin my life a second time, I'll kill you, Dolores. I mean that. I haven't the energy or the desire to start over again at my age and build another career. You bled me of everything I had. If you want to talk to Burbank and tell him who I am, go ahead. You won't gain a penny by it and, if you do, God help you!" It was signed "Hugh."

"And yet," Krill said, "Miss Goody kept telling me over and over that he was not violent. He would get drunk and run away from things he couldn't face. And she knew him as well as anyone."

"He clobbered Judy over the head," Jon pointed out.

"But that was sheer desperation, and I don't think he meant to kill me, just knock me out until he could get away with the briefcase."

"Are you defending the guy?" Krill was half amused, half incredulous.

"He's dead and now I don't believe he killed himself. I'm terribly sorry for him."

Jon looked at her. "Would you have felt that way if he had had the face of a rabbit?"

"Probably not," she admitted.

"Don't," Krill begged, "let a police investigation interfere with these personal exchanges."

Milton looked up. "Brother!" he exclaimed.

"Can you make head or tail of that mess?" Krill asked.

"To be nontechnical—"

"You do that."

"About fifteen years ago Hendricks began to manipulate stocks until he got control not only of coffee but of rubber in the country where he now wants to be ambassador. When I think of the screams that would go up if they knew this—"

"But someone should know," Jon said. "Damn it, we can't send such men abroad to represent us: men who, on the side, are actually pulling strings to control the economy of the country. If you publish that story, where will you stand with your editor?"

Milton scratched his head and began to grin. "We can but put it up to him."

"But look here," Krill said, "Hendricks did not hit Miss Wilkins on the head, steal the briefcase, or kill Allison. He was on a train headed for Washington, D.C., when these things happened."

"What else is there in the briefcase?" Jon asked.

"That's all."

"All?" Jon echoed in dismay. "It can't be. It simply can't be."

Krill fished around inside and then turned the briefcase upside down, thumping the bottom. There was a clink of metal as a small object fell on the desk and he picked up what appeared to be a small cigarette case. He turned it over. "Now what the—" After a moment he lifted the telephone. "Find me Quimmer on the double."

An unexpectedly fat young man with thriving sideburns and thin hair stuck his head around the door. "Want me?"

Krill handed him the small gadget. "Know anything about this?"

"Neat job," Quimmer said in admiration. "Tape recorder. You could carry it in your pocket."

"I imagine that is what was done. Can you get the stuff for me?"

"Sure. Twenty minutes."

While they waited, Milton continued to look through the Hendricks file, which Dolores had stolen. Krill unexpectedly broke down, abandoned officialdom, and talked about the part he was playing in amateur theatricals, though how he was going to get his part memorized when he had to miss so many rehearsals, he didn't know.

Within the allotted time a beaming Quimmer came back with a tape recorder onto which he had threaded a tape. "Took it off our equipment," he explained, started the machine and stood back, listening to the result with a father's pride.

"A mouthwash that really works for hours!" exclaimed a woman's sultry voice in a tone of incredulous surprise.

Judy gave a gasp and sat upright. "That's Dolores," she whispered.

Krill waved for her to be silent.

"My daughter always uses this floor wax," Dolores went on. "So much easier and more efficient than the kind I used to use." There was a brief pause. "When I feel drained of energy, I take one tablespoon or two tablets and, within minutes, I feel youth simply surging through my body."

"Sample commercials to show producers. Like the photographs that models distribute to photographers," Quimmer explained in a low voice.

There were two more brief commercials and then Dolores said, "Who is the pinup?" A man replied, "That's my wifc," and Dolores laughed as a door closed. "No, darling, I'm your wife. I never got around to divorcing you. What the hell! When Gordon refused to marry me, I didn't figure it was worth the expense and the trouble, so I let it drift."

They could hear Burbank's voice as he cursed her. Then Dolores said, "Well, well, are these dear little ones your children? Your little—what's the legal term, Elmer?" Then her voice rose. "Don't touch me! I've really got you where I want you. I can imagine your wife's delight when she finds out that she has been living with you without benefit of clergy."

"I could kill you for this, Doris. Of all the rotten things to do!"

"Don't try it. I need cash, Elmer, and plenty of it. I'm not employable any more, let's face it, and you are in clover. The clover your wife lets you graze in. I want fifty thousand dollars and I want it soon. Three weeks at the outside. You can raise it."

"I'll see you in hell first."

"Better not, my pet. In this briefcase, where I carry —shall I call them my social security documents?—I also have a tape recorder and you're on record, so if anything happens to me . . . Oh, no, you don't. Come one step nearer and I'll scream this place down. Then try to explain. I mean business."

"There's nothing to stop me divorcing you."

"A bit late in the day to please your wife and children, isn't it?"

"I can't raise that kind of money."

"You'll find a way. Otherwise, I have nothing to lose, darling. Nothing at all. If your wife doesn't come across, I'll blow you up in your damned sensitive industry. Trust little Doris."

"You—"

She gave a half laugh, half scream, the door opened and slammed behind her. The tape was silent.

"So Burbank is our man." Krill looked at Jon. "Tell me how you do it—second sight?"

"You mean because I suggested you check to see whether Burbank and Dolores had actually been divorced? No, I just remembered Miss Goody saying Dolores had laughed when he said the picture on the wall was of his wife. I figured that gave him the biggest motive of them all. It meant losing his wife, his job, his family, his standing, his income, everything he valued."

"Valued enough to kill three times?"

"Or four, if necessary. Why do you think we've been doing our best to keep Judy under wraps?"

"First you keep her under wraps, then you dangle her like bait. Make up your mind what you want." Krill lifted the telephone, talked to the Montauk police, then asked for an unmarked car. He got up, shrugged into his jacket, and said, "It's all laid on. They are sending men to make sure Burbank doesn't get away."

"Let me in on this," Milton said. "It will get you in the clear with your department," he added persuasively when the lieutenant hesitated. "I'll give you a nice play. The guy who solved three murders and unearthed a big political scandal."

"Well—" After a moment Krill said, "All right. Come along."

It wasn't until Krill was about to get into the front seat of the car that he saw Judy piling into the back

174

seat with Milton, while Jon tugged fruitlessly at her arm to keep her back. "Hey, you stay where you are!"

"I'm going along," Judy said firmly. "After all, he is my murderer."

Unexpectedly Krill relented. "You may come in useful at that," he said. He added, "For a change."

18

Five o'clock in the morning. Early light dimmed by
fog. The driver of the police car had turned on the de-
mister to clear the windshield and he had switched
from high to low beams.

Now and then, the two policemen in the front seat
exchanged a few words; now and then, the radio spoke
in a mechanical voice. In the back seat Milton slept,
his chin sunk, his breathing heavy.

Once more Jon found Judy's hand conveniently near
and he held it firmly. Gradually her head dropped on
his shoulder and she, too, was asleep.

The "cottage" to which Mrs. Burbank had referred
deprecatingly was a big old-fashioned frame building,
which must have at least twenty rooms. Ugly in archi-
tecture, it had an air of solid comfort and, as the fog
lifted, a breathtaking view.

"It's a hell of a time to expect people to be awake,"
Milton grumbled as he sat up, yawning and rubbing his
eyes.

Judy had waked up as cheerful as a cricket. "Is this
it?" she asked.

"This," Jon told her gravely, "is it," and her smile
faded.

Krill turned around. "You aren't to open your trap.
Is that clear, young woman? And you are to remain in
the car until I need you." As she looked mutinous, he
said, "That's an order, Miss Wilkins," and in response
to his tone she replied meekly, "All right, Lieutenant."

A police car was parked near the house and the
driver got out to speak to Krill. "He is still out fishing,

according to his wife. No sign of him here."

Krill nodded. "Keep an eye on this girl, will you? She's what they call accident-prone." He grinned at Judy and turned toward the entrance, accompanied by his sergeant, Milton, and Jon, the latter joining them only after a last sharp look at Judy to make sure she would stay put.

It was Mrs. Burbank herself who opened the door. She was as neat as though she was always prepared to receive the police at this hour of the morning, her hair beautifully arranged, wearing a trim blue skirt and a white silk shirt, a blue cashmere sweater over her shoulders.

She looked at the four men who waited at the door, said, "Good morning, gentlemen," without surprise, and stood back to let them enter. She indicated a big glass-enclosed room on the right, a chintzy room, filled with comfortable furniture.

"I am sorry to disturb you at this time," Krill said uncomfortably. A three-time killer was the kind of person he was glad to put out of the way, but families were different. The ones who were innocent were the ones who suffered.

Mrs. Burbank, however, seemed to be in complete command of herself and of the situation. "I've been expecting you," she said, "ever since your call. Anyhow, dear Goody—"

Miss Goody nodded briefly to them from a nearby chair. She looked in surprise at Jon. "Mr. Fullbright, isn't it?"

Krill performed introductions. There was a moment of strained silence and then Mrs. Burbank said, too brightly, too casually, "Goody said you would probably be here early." She swallowed convulsively and Jon noticed how pale she was under the careful make-up, how shadowed her eyes were. "I didn't like to awaken the servants, as they have to keep fairly long hours in the summer season. Anyhow, there was no reason for letting them know—uh—Goody made some coffee and there are doughnuts."

177

She waved them to chairs. "Thank you, ma'am," Krill said. "We'd appreciate the coffee. Is Mr. Burbank joining us?"

"He'll be here any time now," she said brightly, a fingernail scratching at the upholstery on the arm of her chair.

"You're sure of that?" the lieutenant asked sharply.

"He went out fishing early yesterday morning. As a rule he is gone for several days at a time on these expeditions. So relaxing for him. I think that's important when a man's job demands a great deal of nervous strain. But we have an emergency signal we worked out years ago when one of the children had a bad accident and I couldn't reach Elmer. A flag is flown on the Point where he can see it when he uses his binoculars. Of course in the dark it would not be visible, but now that it is light he'll pick it up and be in at once."

"Do relax," Miss Goody said, and her voice was gentle. "I'll serve coffee for these men, Hazel. You leave it to me."

Jon went to help her and distributed coffee, cream and sugar, a plate of doughnuts. Mrs. Burbank shook her head when he brought her a cup.

"How bad is it?" Miss Goody asked him in a low tone.

Jon shrugged his shoulders.

"That story in the paper about Doris being a blackmailer. Was it true?" She wasn't one to waste time in getting to the point.

He nodded.

"Someone really killed her? She didn't just fall off the subway platform?"

"We think—that is, the police think—that she was deliberately killed."

"Do you believe it was Elmer Burbank?"

Jon was silent.

"That whole story about the pretty girl you had with you at the office, the one who was supposed to have murdered her roommate for her money, the one who got twenty-four hours from the police to produce a briefcase—what was the truth in all that rigamarole?"

"That was the briefcase for which Dolores Costanza was murdered," Jon said, and Mrs. Burbank's head jerked around as though it were on strings. "It contained the incriminating stuff she was using for blackmail."

"I always knew she was a bad one," Miss Goody said.

Lieutenant Krill set down his coffee cup and got to his feet. "I am sorry, Mrs. Burbank, but I have a search warrant."

She moistened her lips. "Of course. I wouldn't dream of interfering with the law. Though I hope it won't be necessary to disturb the children." She moistened her lips again. "Why are you doing this, Lieutenant?"

There was no advantage in softening these things. "We believe that Mr. Burbank is guilty of three murders."

"No!" It wasn't a cry, it wasn't a whimper, just a breath. "No!"

Miss Goody came to stand beside her, to reach for her wrist, feel her pulse. "Did you have to do it like that?"

"But they are wrong, Goody," Mrs. Burbank said. "You know Elmer. He couldn't do such a thing. Not Elmer."

After asking which rooms Mr. Burbank occupied, Krill and his sergeant started upstairs. Mrs. Burbank turned from Milton to Jon as though seeking reassurance. "There must be some terrible mistake. Elmer is too sensible. He wouldn't kill anyone who tried to blackmail him."

"A blackmailer never stops," the reporter said.

"But even if there was something—wrong—in Elmer's past, he knows I—he could have whatever he wanted. He knows that!"

"You told me yourself," Jon reminded her, "that,

like your father, you would never submit to blackmail."

"But if the alternative was—was killing someone, I couldn't hesitate."

"It might depend on why he was being blackmailed. There might be something on which you would refuse to support him."

"All this is ridiculous. I've called my lawyer and he will be here this morning. I told him I didn't believe there could be anything serious, but Elmer has been fishing so much lately, night fishing too, that it might be hard for him to establish an alibi." Her fingernail had torn a hole in the upholstery; now she worked at it, enlarged it. "What are they looking for?"

"I don't know," Jon admitted. "Probably a rifle, among other things."

"A rifle!"

"An attempt was made to kill Miss Wilkins and me and get hold of the briefcase. Someone had a rifle and shot the wrong person in the dark. I think he panicked; at any rate, he didn't wait to carry out his plan."

"I don't believe Elmer ever owned a rifle. He doesn't like hunting. He doesn't like killing things. Except fish. And fish are different, after all."

Jon made no answer, but he accepted another cup of coffee.

"Will the men be out of the house before the children are awake?" Mrs. Burbank asked. "I don't want them to be involved in any of this unpleasantness."

The word seemed hardly adequate, but Jon realized that, in spite of her anxiety and distress, Mrs. Burbank was sure that as soon as her family lawyer arrived everything would be all right, restored to its usual pleasantness, that nothing could distrub, let alone disrupt, her safe world. Seeing Miss Goody's expression, he was aware that she took a different view. She would not be surprised by any disclosures concerning Elmer Burbank, nor, apparently, much upset by them, except for their repercussions on the younger woman who was probably home and family and children to her. Jon was glad that when the inevitable exposure came,

180

Mrs. Burbank would have Miss Goody's unswerving loyalty and staunch support.

"Mr. Fullbright," Mrs. Burbank said, "there were other people being blackmailed by Doris, weren't there?"

"Including your—uh, Mr. Burbank, there were four men and one woman that we know of. There may, of course, have been more."

"But what about the others?"

"None of them could have committed all these murders or made the attacks on Miss Wilkins to regain the briefcase."

"Does she have it?"

"No," Jon said quietly, "the police have it, Mrs.— uh, Burbank."

Well, he had dropped two hints. It was Miss Goody who understood first. She stood protectively beside the woman whom she had watched grow up, of whom she was so fond.

And then, belatedly, the younger woman suspected. "No," she whispered. She looked at Jon and color flooded her cheeks, drained from them. "You've been trying to suggest something. You hesitated before you said my husband, before you called me Mrs. Burbank. Are you trying to suggest that Elmer wasn't divorced from that woman, that we aren't really married?"

Jon nodded.

"Oh, my God! The children. The children! How could he do that to them?"

"He didn't know. He never knew until she came to his office just before she was killed. She told him then. She hadn't got a divorce because the other man wouldn't marry her. I don't know whether she was aware of Burbank's marriage to you or whether it didn't matter until she was really desperate for money. A woman on the verge of starvation or going on relief, her career ended, can easily be ruthless as a matter of survival."

"But the children!"

Miss Goody's voice, sharp, impersonal, efficient, was

a bracer for the distraught mother. "Mr. Fullbright, how did the police get hold of the briefcase?"

Jon described how it had been gotten rid of by Judy in a panic after both Dolores and Peg Morrison had been killed for it, how it had been traced to a moving van in Indianapolis, and they had flown there the evening before to retrieve it.

"Then the police never really suspected Miss Wilkins," Miss Goody said.

"Not after the second attempt had been made to murder her," Jon said.

"That was—Elmer?"

Jon made no comment.

"But Elmer is out fishing," Mrs. Burbank said. "He'll be in soon. He can explain. No matter what this Miss Wilkins says—where is she, anyhow?"

"Outside, waiting in a police car," Jon said. "Under guard."

"You need not be afraid for her here. Hadn't you better bring her in? She'll want coffee." Mrs. Burbank added bitterly, "Elmer isn't here to hurt her, so there's nothing to be afraid of."

Jon went out of the room, onto the circular driveway. The police car was gone and so was the unmarked car. There was no sign of Judy.

II

She had fallen asleep in the back of the car, curled up on the seat. Dimly she was aware of the monotonous, metallic radio voice in the police car. Then the motor roared and the car moved off. She stirred sleepily, but before she was fully awake, the door of the driver's seat of the unmarked car was opened and a man slid under the wheel. He started the car, moved down the driveway. She saw the broad shoulders, the profile. Elmer Burbank.

She sat up abruptly and reached for the door. At the

same moment he saw her in his rear-view mirror and swore. He put on speed.

"I wouldn't if I were you. You God-damned little snooper." There was no anger in his voice. It was flat and matter-of-fact. "I'm not going to hurt you. Just tell me what I want to know and I'll let you go."

"You've already murdered three people. You've tried twice to kill me. Why should I believe you?"

"Is that what the police think?"

"That's what they think." Queerly enough, she wasn't frightened. Now that there was no place to hide, now that she had been trapped, she felt clear-headed and calm. "This is just silly, you know. How far do you think you can get in a stolen police car, even if it's unmarked? You'll be stopped any minute now. As soon as they finish your house, they will find that you have stolen their car and kidnapped me."

"What are they searching for?"

"Among other things, a rifle."

He laughed, passed another car, touching the siren as he did so, and laughed again as the car ahead hastily pulled to one side. "The rifle is now deep, deep in the water. What else?"

"I don't know. The important thing is that we found Dolores Costanza's briefcase. It's really no use, Mr. Burbank."

"And what was in the briefcase?"

"Among other things, a tape recording of your interview with Miss—with your wife."

"My wife." Automatically the car accelerated as his foot pressed on the gas, and then slowed as he realized the powerful car was out of control. "So that's that." He asked almost quietly, "Does my—does Hazel know?"

"I wasn't inside. But she has probably been told by now."

"I guess that does it. All that for nothing. For this. It's the one thing Hazel would never forgive. Because of the kids. But, good God, she can't believe I

183

would have done that to them deliberately. I honestly thought I was free to marry her. There must be some way of convincing her." He seemed to be talking to himself rather than to Judy.

"But it isn't that easy, Mr. Burbank," she told him sadly. "This isn't just a question of getting squared off with your—with Mrs. Burbank. You killed Dolores Costanza and then you smashed Peg Morrison's skull because you thought she had the right briefcase. You were as ruthless as though she didn't count at all as long as your comfortable life was safe. When people feel like that, think that other people's lives don't count, then they are really dangerous. You tried to smother me when you thought I had the case, and you shot Rogers just because you saw someone against the light and took a chance that it was I, coming to Jon's house for protection, or Jon himself. You didn't really care, did you? You deliberately caused an accident that might have killed two state policemen when their car overturned. And then you poisoned poor Hugh Allison. In a way, that's the worst thing you did. Your wife nearly smashed his life and then you —just ended it."

"Once I'd taken the briefcase from him, what else could I do? He knew who I was. I followed you to that little house in the Village after Fullbright's maid told me where you expected to go and that you had a briefcase. I saw this guy in the lobby, though I didn't know then he was Bennett."

"And anyhow it wouldn't have mattered to you if he got in your way."

"The funny thing," Burbank said, "is that I got that cyanide pill for myself. Got it a long time ago from a guy in the CIA who had it for his own last resort. He was quitting because he was sick of cloak and dagger work. I bought it from him as a—well, you never know. Cancer or something. But then I gave myself away to Bennett, to Allison. I didn't seem to plan anything. I wandered around behind him. I just leaned over and forced the cyanide pill into his mouth. Wasted it on him."

"Wasted," Judy said thoughtfully. "You've gone a long way outside the human race, haven't you, Mr. Burbank?"

"That's not true. I've always been a good mixer, a good guy. I get along with people. I never wanted any rough stuff. I hate it. But—what could I do?"

"What do you think you'll do now, Mr. Burbank? That's the important thing."

"I'm going to cut my losses. I'm losing the works: Hazel and the kids and my home and job and prestige. But I'm not a complete damned fool. I have a second line of defense. The day I saw Dolores in the office, I began to make plans. I have another car and another license and another name at a New York garage, and enough money in traveler's checks to keep me going for a long time."

"If it weren't for Peg and Hugh Allison, I might have let you go," Judy said. "But Peg never knew anything about it. She was the innocent bystander. You just brushed her out of the way and smashed her as though she were a—a moth."

Burbank laughed. "You're a cute little trick, but you've got the brains of a day-old chick. So you might have 'let' me go."

There was a siren behind them. "That's for you," she said. "It was bound to come, sooner or later."

"Don't try bluffing me, sister, or taking my mind off my driving. This car has the kick of a mule. You just sit tight, and when we get to Manhattan I'll release you, safe and sound."

"It's too late. One day, Peg and I were on the Garden State Parkway and she asked for a map. There's a way you open it so it reads: HELP. I've been holding it out of the window. Peg was amused and gave it to me to keep off prowlers. I'm sort of glad you're being caught with something Peg gave me, Mr. Burbank."

A police car passed, pulled in front. Another was at

185

the side, siren going, lights blinking. Burbank braked, pulled over to the side. The policemen converged on the car, their guns drawn.

III

Elmer Burbank, white and silent, was removed in the first police car. The second man, after talking over his two-way radio, came back to speak to Judy.

"You all right, miss?"

"Yes."

"Did he threaten you?"

"He wanted to find out what the police knew. He said he was going to release me in Manhattan, safe and sound."

"Did you believe him?"

"Yes, I think I did."

"From the story I got, he tried to kill you more than once."

"But there was nothing more to gain. He was throwing in his hand. And he has another car and license and money in traveler's checks he has been getting together ever since Dolores—since his wife told him he wasn't divorced and that his children were illegitimate. I think he knew if he couldn't find that tape recorder he would be all washed up."

There was a siren and another police car drew up. Krill, his sergeant, Milton, and Jon all tumbled out. The sergeant who had left the keys in the car was rather red. Jon was white. At something in his expression Judy decided it would be the better part of valor to keep still.

They drove to police headquarters, where she was asked to tell her story in detail. When she had finished and signed her statement, Krill said she was free to go until she was called upon to testify. If, he added darkly, she could keep out of trouble that long.

"I'll be responsible for her," Jon said, "if I have to keep her handcuffed."

186

For the first time in twenty-four hours the exhausted Krill managed a laugh. "There are better ways. At least, so I've been told."

Jon steered her out of the police station, still in grim silence, hailed a taxi.

"Where are we going?" she asked at last.

"My doctor."

"Are you hurt?" she asked in alarm.

"Blood tests. And then it takes three days."

After a moment's shock she asked, rather breathlessly, "Aren't you taking a lot for granted?"

"Am I? Am I, Judy?"

"You don't know anything about me except that I keep getting you into trouble and taking your mind off your work."

"So you do."

"I can't even cook very well."

"There are restaurants."

"And what about Benedick the bachelor?"

"I love you. This is serious with me. And you ought to marry me right away; there's such a lot to catch up on."

"Like what?"

"Like what kind of girl you are when you don't have to hide. Like whether you eat your steak rare or well done. Like whether you're Republican or Democrat. Like how well we get on together. A lot of things and only one lifetime for them."

"Then," she agreed, "let's not waste any more time."

The taxi driver looked in his rear-view mirror, raised his eyebrows. Wow! He pulled in at the curb. "I hate to break that up," he said politely. "This is the number you wanted, mister."

"You bet it is!" Jon agreed.

How many of these Dell bestsellers have you read?

THE SENSUOUS WOMAN by "J" $1.25

DELIVERANCE by James Dickey $1.25

BALL FOUR by Jim Bouton $1.25

THE ANDERSON TAPES by Lawrence Sanders $1.25

MARY QUEEN OF SCOTS by Antonia Fraser $1.50

THE AMERICAN HERITAGE DICTIONARY   75c

MILE HIGH by Richard Condon $1.25

THE VALUE OF NOTHING by John Weitz $1.25

THE ESTATE by Isaac Bashevis Singer $1.25

PATTON by Ladislas Farago $1.25

THE ANDROMEDA STRAIN by Michael Crichton $1.25

THE POSEIDON ADVENTURE by Paul Gallico $1.25

THE DOCTOR'S QUICK WEIGHT LOSS DIET by Irwin M. Stillman, M. D. and Samm Sinclair Baker   95c

SOUL ON ICE by Eldridge Cleaver   95c

THE $20,000,000 HONEYMOON by Fred Sparks   95c